Friendly Wonder Guide

Vol 2

TOGAF® 10 Level 1

TOGAF® Enterprise Architecture

Exam Part 1

(Foundation) Certification Preparation

Table of Contents

Largest bank of Questions, Answers with detailed Explanation of how the answer is arrived at. Do great at Level 1 Certification and go beyond with initial preparation for Level 2 with this Book Volumes

True TOGAF® Enterprise Architecture Part 1 Exam treatment for TOGAF® 10, all updates to TOGAF® 10 version duly incorporated. TOGAF® 10 is considered to be a 'difficult one' by a few.

We feel it is quite 'different' but not 'difficult'. Our Book Series on Friendly Wonder Guide proves that.

We have published Wonder Guides for TOGAF® 9.2 since long, and they are quite popular. While TOGAF® 9.2 Certification still continues to be available, what could be the difference in taking TOGAF® 10 Exam, which are incidentally known as Enterprise Architecture Certification and not by a version number ?

Note that TOGAF® 10 has an upgraded Exam syllabus content that spans into the Core document - TOGAF® Standard Fundamental Content Version 10

and a little into a few Series Guides that are added in the Exam Conformance list.

Thus, the knowledge base with it is broader, with a number of state-of-art topics well highlighted through the Series Guides.

Hence, the value behind the Certificate goes up when it is on TOGAF® 10.

We have taken care of referring to those contents from Series Guides that seem to be important for TOGAF® 10 Certification. Our Books on Level 2 Exam steps into additional focus here, since questions may expect acknowledge of appropriate portions of some of the Series Guides.

Also note that **Illustration based – Pictur**

e (image) centric questions are common in Level 1 Exam of TOGAF® 10. We have done enough justice in including such questions which are possibly relating to corresponding images that are part of TOGAF® standard documentation. You will see many such questions in this multi-volume series.

A further point to note is about the **table-style questions** in Level 1 Exam of TOGAF® 10. These often test your knowledge across ADM or across the breadth of TOGAF® by mixing up with points which lie across the syllabus content. We have added quite a number of such questions and the explanation therein will prepare you for tackling such questions with confidence.

There are **Twin stage questions**, in the style of '**match this to that**' which can also appear in Level 1 Exam. We cover such questions also in these multiple volumes, with explanatory approach as to how you can encounter them with ease.

This multi-Volume Series refers to TOGAF® 10 :The free-standing documents of TOGAF® Standard Fundamental Content :

Introduction and Core Concepts

Architecture Development Method

ADM Techniques

Applying ADM

Architecture Content

Enterprise Architecture Capability and Governance

As also from TOGAF® Series Guides of :

A Practitioners' Approach to Developing Enterprise Architecture Following the TOGAF® ADM

The TOGAF® Leader's Guide to Establishing and Evolving an EA Capability

Enabling Enterprise Agility

Integrating Risk and Security within a TOGAF® Enterprise Architecture

Business Scenarios

Using the TOGAF® Standard in the Digital Enterprise

Books in this Friendly Wonder Guide Series include :

Friendly Wonder Guide Part I

Module 1 : Introduction and Core concepts of TOGAF®

Module 2 : Preliminary Phase of ADM

Module 3 : Phase A : Architecture Vision

Module 4 : Requirement Management Phase

Module 5 : Phase B : Business Architecture

Friendly Wonder Guide Part III

Module 14 : Phase E : Opportunities and Solutions

Module 15 : Phase F : Migration Planning

Module 16 : Phase G : Implementation Governance

Module 17 : Phase H : Change Management

Module 18 : Architecture Governance

And *enhancement Modules of :*

Module 19 : Enhancements over Introduction and Core concepts

Module 20 : Enhancements over Preliminary Phase

Module 21 : Enhancements over Phase A

Module 22 : Enhancements over Requirements Management

Module 23 : Enhancements over Phase B

Module 24 : Enhancements over View, Viewpoints and Building Blocks ; Content Management Framework

Module 25 : Enhancements over Phase C : Application Architecture

Module 26 : Enhancements over Phase C : Data Architecture

Module 27 : Enhancements over Phase D

Module 28 : Enhancements over Architecture Partitioning

Module 29 : Enhancements over Foundation and higher Architectures

Module 30 : Enhancements over Architecture Repository

Module 31 : Enhancements over Enterprise Continuum

Module 32 : Risk Management

Section numbers appearing in explanation refer to respective **TOGAF® 10 documentation**.

We have quoted many phrases and sentences and sections from TOGAF® documentation as a means of better understanding of the subject, especially from Level 1 Certification viewpoint. Often additional words or explanatory substitutions of words and phrases are inserted thereon to ease your understanding. Relevant sections of it are referred to in the Explanation portion of questions herein. TOGAF® 10 documentation can be accessed at : https://pubs.opengroup.org/TOGAF®-standard/[1]

Same portion of TOGAF® documentation may repeat under Explanation portion of different questions. This is done to treat each question as one open for random study also. It is not compulsory to start at a Module and go through each question in a sequential manner.

Does this Book help only towards Level 1 (Foundation) Certification Examination ? The Questions and Answers in this book do serve that purpose very well.

The complete syllabus for Part 1 Certification learning and Exam is seen as one portion of the document, available at : https://publications.opengroup.org/x2202

Do note that apart from TOGAF® standard documentation, a few TOGAF® Series Guides are mentioned as part of learning and Exam syllabus. This Series Guides on TOGAF® 10 Certification take due cognizance of this and has provided justice therein.

The Explanation that appears for each question serves three purposes

1) In understanding the **reason for something being correct answer in Level 1**. Such a reasoning will help you answer any other similar or related question that will appear in Level 1 Certification Examination.

2) Since it refers to relevant sections in the TOGAF® documentation bundle, when you move onto **preparing for Level 2 Certification Examination**, you will be able to navigate to the relevant portion of Scenario based questions with ease with the open book bundle that appears on the Examination Screen. Quick navigation will be one of the success formula in any Open Book Exam.

3) Your good understanding of TOGAF® with these Explanation sections will be of high degree of **help during subsequent engagement with Enterprise Architecture at work, in interviews and so on**.

When we refer to TOGAF® in this page and elsewhere in this book, we actually mean **TOGAF®. All Trademarks and TOGAF® including Boundaryless Information Flow™ are respected and is implied to have applied where applicable.**

Module 6 : View, Viewpoints and Building Blocks

Note that questions do come up with answer choices and correct answer picked up from other modules beyond these. Revisit all questions after revising the whole of TOGAF®.

Cross References shown as 'See' herein refer to the **3. Architectural Artifacts**[1] or **5. Building Blocks**[2] under Architecture Content part of TOGAF® Standard Fundamental Content Version 10

In case any other free-standing document of TOGAF® Standard Fundamental Content Version 10 or Series Guide is referenced, that is explicitly mentioned.

Q 601 In the view creation process, the viewpoints are selected based on who's / which concerns ?

A. Architect

B. Stakeholder

C. Views

D. Architecture

Explanation :

Concerns come from stakeholders and Architect is expected to address them.

See under : **3.2.2 Architecture View Creation Process**[3] : under 3.2 Developing Architecture Views in the ADM

The architect may ...... a new ....viewpoint that will cover the ... from it : Can choose any point of view (Viewpoint). Subsequently View preparation (meaning producing various artifact Building Blocks and any other deliverable documents and also adding suitably to Architecture Requirement Specification) is taken up. These are ideally done through steps of the Phases, especially in Phases B to D where the ABBs take shape.

Whatever the context, the architect should be .... has an ..., at least ..., and that .... viewpoint in a systematic way will ...; i.e., does ... concerns ? : See the correlation between View and Viewpoint. The 'systematic way' is by following steps of the Phases. Various Reviews (Peer Revies, Stakeholder Review) are used during the steps to assess the effectiveness.

Also see under : **1.1 Executive Overview : What specifically would prompt the development of an Enterprise Architecture ?**[4] : under Introduction and Core Concepts part of TOGAF® Standard Fundamental Content Version 10

What specifically .... of an Enterprise ... ? : : What initiates the 'review or 'development' ? In connection with what kind of transformation ? Also think why these are necessitated. Why is it called 'to manage complexity' ?

---

1. https://pubs.opengroup.org/togaf-standard/architecture-content/chap03.html

2. https://pubs.opengroup.org/togaf-standard/architecture-content/chap05.html

3. https://pubs.opengroup.org/togaf-standard/architecture-content/chap03.html#tag_03_02_02

4. https://pubs.opengroup.org/togaf-standard/introduction/chap01.html#tag_01_01_00_04

Often key people identify .... Such people are commonly referred to as the ".... Note how Stakeholders are mentioned as 'key people'.

The role of the architect is to ... by :

▪ Identifying and ... the requirements that the ... have : What is done with the 'requirement' here ?

▪ Developing ... architecture that show how the ... are going to be .... : Developing what and to show what ?

▪ Showing the .... in reconciling the .... stakeholders : When does the need for trade-offs arise ?

Without the ....Architecture, it is highly unlikely that all ... will be .... and ...: Get to know the importance of Enterprise Architecture here.

(Serious learners are advised to refer to TOGAF® documentation of section – such as the one referred to here - in the online link : https://pubs.opengroup.org/TOGAF®-standard/[5])

Answer : B

———————

Q 602 Which of the following are all steps View Creation Process ?

A. Select Key Stakeholders

B. Select Appropriate Viewpoints

C. Refer existing viewpoint from library

D. Create viewpoints from artifacts

E. A, B and D

F. B, C and D

G. A, B and C

(Only for practicing purposes. Usually Exam questions start with D or so and will not have the multiple grouping like what is shown here in E, F and G)

Explanation :

Understanding these steps is important, since that is what an Architect is expected to do in course of ADM.

See under : **3.2.2 Architecture View Creation Process**[6]

It will often be possible to create the ..... for a particular architecture by following ..... : Get to know each of these and try to relate to steps of Phases B to D. Creating Views is the process, meaning following the steps, in order to come out with 'Views' which are nothing but all that is produced by the Architect – Artifact Building Blocks and all other deliverable documents as the supporting work pieces.

5. https://pubs.opengroup.org/togaf-standard/

6. https://pubs.opengroup.org/togaf-standard/architecture-content/chap03.html#tag_03_02_02

1. Refer ... viewpoints : What all to refer, from where (Hint – Architecture Repository and Enterprise Continuum)

2. Select ... viewpoints (based on the ... and .... by views) : Based on what ?

3. Generate .... the system by using the ... as templates : Select what, and then to do what ?

Also see under : **3.3.2 Identify Stakeholders, Concerns, and Business Requirements : Step From Phase A : Architecture Vision**[7]

Identify the .... and their .... and define the . ...requirements to be ..... engagement : How are key business requirement defined ?

Answer : G

———————

Q 603 Which of the following is considered by TOGAF® as a MAJOR attribute of a good Building Block ?

A. A Building Block that is re-usable

B. A Building Block meeting business needs

C. A Building Block with public interfaces

D. A Building Block that guides the development of solutions

E. A Building Block that is product-aware

Explanation :

TOGAF® places a lot of importance on one specific aspect of every Building Block – it should be as much re-usable as possible. TOGAF® considers re-usability as an attribute of a good Building Block.

When an architect is developing an architecture, such a person does not work with real components, but works rather with descriptions of idealised components, called Building Blocks.

ABB and SBB are basically terminology used by TOGAF® for defining discrete Building Block Components of Enterprise Architecture. Building Blocks in turn can be defined at different levels of detail, depending on the stage or Phase of ADM.

See **1.1 Overview**[8] : 1. Introduction under Architecture Content part of TOGAF® Standard Fundamental Content Version 10

: Building Blocks can be defined ....., depending on what stage of architecture development has been reached. For instance, at an ......, a Building Block ..... Later on, a Building Block may be ..... Building Blocks can .... : Building Blocks can be seen at different levels of detail and that depends on the ADM Phase; can be an outline (in Phase A) and may develop into ABB Components in Phases B to D and then into multiple layers of Transition blocks culminating in SBBs in Phase E.

---

7. https://pubs.opengroup.org/togaf-standard/adm/chap03.html#tag_03_03_02

8. https://pubs.opengroup.org/togaf-standard/architecture-content/chap01.html#tag_01_01

— **Architecture Building Blocks (ABBs)** typically describe .... : ABBs describe what ? Which may be included in them ?

— **Solution Building Blocks (SBBs)** represent .... : SBBS – how are they connected with realization ? What is the capability seen therein ?

Answer : A

———————

Q 604 Which among the following statements is NOT correct ?

A. TOGAF® recommends the exact way in which functionality, products, and custom developments are assembled into Building Blocks

B. Every organization must decide for itself what arrangement of Building Blocks works best for it

C. A good choice of Building Blocks can lead to improvements in legacy system integration, interoperability, and flexibility in the creation of new systems and applications

D. An architecture is a composition of a set of Building Blocks and the specification of how those Building Blocks are connected

E. Various Building Blocks in an architecture specify the services required in an enterprise specific system

Explanation :

TOGAF® **does not recommend the exact way** Building Blocks are assembled. Every organization must decide for itself what arrangement of Building Blocks works best for it. It may even change a little from project to project at architecture level and vary from solution approach to solution approach at technology level.

See under : **5.2.2 Generic Characteristics**[9] : 5. Building Blocks under Architecture Content part of TOGAF® Standard Fundamental Content Version 10

A Building Block's ... should be loosely coupled to its ... i.e., it should be .... without impacting the ... of the building block : What are the things to be loosely coupled ? What is means by 'realizing in different ways' ?

The level of detail to which a ... be specified is dependent on the ... and, in some cases, less ... greater value (for example, ... has more value than ...). :ote the dependencies mentioned.

The way in which .... are assembled into building blocks will vary widely between ..... Every organization .... what arrangement of ... best for it. A good choice of building blocks can lead to .... in the creation of .... : What are the variations mentioned here, that can vary from Enterprise to Enterprise ? What is the advantage in choosing Building Blocks wisely ?

Also see : **5.3.1.1 Building Blocks in Architecture Design**[10] : 5. Building Blocks under Architecture Content part of TOGAF® Standard Fundamental Content Version 10

---

9. https://pubs.opengroup.org/togaf-standard/architecture-content/chap05.html#tag_05_02_02

10. https://pubs.opengroup.org/togaf-standard/architecture-content/chap05.html#tag_05_03_01_01

An architecture is a set of .... depicted in an ..., and a .... how those ... are connected to ... of the business : What is the 'depicted in' that is indicate here ?

Answer : A

———————————

Q 605 Complete the sentence by selecting the applicable pair of words. According to TOGAF®, a / an _____ is used to describe the ____ of a stakeholder.

A. activity model, perspective

B. viewpoint, requirements

C. view, concerns

D. Node Connectivity Diagram, interconnections

E. Architecture trade-off analysis, constraints

Explanation :

TOGAF® makes it very clear that a view is used to describe the concerns of a stakeholder.

See under : **3.4.2 : Architecture Views and Architecture Viewpoints in Enterprise Architecture** [11]

The users of the system have an ... that reflects their ..., and the ....of the system have a different .... Architecture .... to address ... of the two architecture ...are unlikely to ...., because ... how each ... : User of a system – what Viewpoint and how is it different from the Viewpoints of other stakeholders mentioned here ? So, what is done to address it ? (Hint : 'views that are developed'). Why is a mention of' 'unlikely' here ?

On incorrect answer choices :

Answer choice A) : activity model, perspective : More relevant to Business Architecture, not to all stakeholders.

Answer choice B) : related viewpoint to requirements, not to stakeholders.

Answer choice D) : Node Connectivity Diagram, interconnections : More relevant to Technology Architecture.

Answer choice E) : Architecture trade-off analysis, constraints : Relate to the way suggested requirements are taken to further details.

Answer : C

---

11. https://pubs.opengroup.org/togaf-standard/architecture-content/chap03.html#tag_03_04_02

Q 606 Complete the sentence. According to TOGAF®, a view is a representation of a system from the perspective of the _____ of a stakeholder.

A. concerns

B. constraints

C. interests

D. perspective

E. requirements

Explanation :

View is a representation of a system from the perspective of the concerns of a stakeholder.

The View Creation process is also about selecting the appropriate architecture viewpoints (based on the stakeholders and concerns that need to be covered by views).

See : **3.1 Basic Concepts**[12]

An "architecture view" is a ... of a system from the ... of a related set of .... It consists of one or more .... of the system. An "Architecture ..." is a representation of a ... A model ... a ...scale, ..., and/or ... representation of the .... In ... or ... the design of a ..., the architect will typically create ...., possibly using ... An architecture view will comprise ... of one or .., chosen so as to .. or .. that their .... in the ... of the system .. : View - representation of a system, stakeholder (concern) perspective; View is made up of models. from the perspective of a related set of concerns. It consists of one or more architecture models of the system. Get to know here more about the concept of model. Get to see how design and architecture are tied down to models. How does the architect choose the models and views ?

On incorrect answer choices :

Answer choice B) : Organizational constraints, Budget information, Financial constraints, External constraints and Business constraints : these are not Views but are restrictions imposed on the architecture.

Answer choice C) : Interests : Actually "concerns" are interests in a system relevant to one or more of its stakeholders and not of "a" stakeholder. This is a near correct answer.

Answer choice D) : Perspective : Obviously a Perspective cannot be "a representation of a system from the perspective".

Answer choice E) : Requirements : These are based on need and are to be addressed in the architecture engagement. It comes out of the system need and is not the "representation of a system".

Views lead to description of the perspective. Perspectives are just 'guides' in the process. **Viewpoint** defines the Perspective.

Answer : A

_____

12. **https://pubs.opengroup.org/togaf-standard/architecture-content/chap03.html#tag_03_01**

Q 607 Which of these is not a recommended step to create the required views for a particular architecture ?

A. Refer to any existing libraries of viewpoints

B. Select key stakeholders

C. Analyze their requirement and document them

D. Select appropriate viewpoints

E. Get views of the system using the selected viewpoints as templates

Explanation :

Analyze their requirement and document them is not a step that is specifically mentioned and recommended under View Creation Process. It related to couple of steps that are part of Phases B, C and D.

For example, we see under : **4.5.1 General**[13] about how analysing the requirement is done in Phase B etc., as part of the "architectural work" step and not view creation process step :

Gather and analyze .....

This is at 4. Business Architecture[14] under Architecture Development Method part of TOGAF® Standard Fundamental Content Version 10

These are part of following steps in Phases B, C and D :

Perform gap analysis

Define candidate roadmap components

Resolve impacts across the Architecture Landscape

Conduct formal stakeholder review

Finalize the Business Architecture

Create the Architecture Definition Document

See under : **3.2.2 Architecture View Creation Process**[15]

It will often be possible to ... by following these steps :

1. Refer to ...

2. Select the ..

3. Generate ..

Answer : C

---

13. https://pubs.opengroup.org/togaf-standard/adm/chap04.html#tag_04_05_01

14. https://pubs.opengroup.org/togaf-standard/adm/chap04.html

15. https://pubs.opengroup.org/togaf-standard/architecture-content/chap03.html#tag_03_02_02

Q 608 What does Architecture Building Blocks do as compared to Solution Building Blocks ?

A. They define how the functionality will be realized through products and components

B. They capture architecture requirements

C. They define the implementation

D. They fulfil business requirements

E. They are product or vendor-aware

Explanation :

Architecture Building Blocks[16] (ABBs) take off from a Superior Architecture.[17] They stop by describing the required capability and they are the architectural basis for shaping the SBBs later on.

See this in **5.5 Where are ABBs?**

and **5.3 Operating in the Context of Superior Architecture**

<u>TOGAF® Series Guide : A Practitioners' Approach to Developing Enterprise Architecture Following the TOGAF® ADM</u>[18]

For example, a ordering services capability in an eCommerce may be required within an enterprise, supported by many SBBs, such as selection using suitable UI on a platform such as Web or Mobile (Android or iPhone, handling data to and from a brand name store (specific RDBMS product such as SQL Server version Z, Message Queue in Kafka running in XYZ Cloud and so on), and application software (Kubernetes on AWS cloud vendor service).

ABBs stop with platform independent model of the architecture and so stops as soon as the requirements are captured and get expressed as Architectural artifacts. This happens mostly during Phases B, C and D.

SBBs are worked on during Phase E. They are created to describe the ABB into solution terms with platform dependant and vendor aware architectural design.

<u>**5.2.3 Architecture Building Blocks**</u>[19]

Architecture Building Blocks (ABBs) relate ..., and are ...of the ADM.

5.2.3.1 Characteristics : ABBs :

▪ Capture ...

▪ Direct and guide ..

5.2.3.2 Specification Content :

---

16. https://pubs.opengroup.org/togaf-standard/adm-practitioners/adm-practitioners_5.html#_Toc95288843

17. https://pubs.opengroup.org/togaf-standard/adm-practitioners/adm-practitioners_5.html#_Toc95288841

18. https://pubs.opengroup.org/togaf-standard/adm-practitioners/index.html

19. https://pubs.opengroup.org/togaf-standard/architecture-content/chap05.html#tag_05_02_03

Fundamental ... and .. - .., unambiguous, including ... and .. : Functional ones such as semantic logic and NFRs – Non Functional Requirements (examples given here being security, capability and manageability.

▪ Interfaces - ..., ... : How to connect with one another, through exposed interface and asking interface.

▪ .... and .... with other .. : Aiming at maximum interoperability, say leading to highly sharable microservices.

▪ Dependent .... with ... and ... : All round dependability so that functionality is wider, broadcast in service registries with well recognizable names.

▪ Map to .... entities and ... : Business to IT alignment.

Answer : B

————————

Q 609 Which one of the following statements about TOGAF® Building Blocks is true ?

A. Building Blocks at a functional level are known as Solutions Building Blocks

B. Solutions Building Blocks are selected in Phases A, B, C and D

C. The specification of a Building Block should be loosely coupled to its implementation

D. The gap analysis technique should be used to identify Building Blocks for re-use

Explanation :

On incorrect answer choices :

Answer choice A) : Functional level is ABB.

Answer choice B) : We get into SBB only ideally at Phase E.

Answer choice D) : Reuse possibility is checked at steps prior to : Perform Gap Analysis.

What do we mean by "loosely coupled to its implementation" ?

It means that the ABB must reveal what is to be implemented. without insisting on how it will be implemented. This is achievable by suitable abstraction, especially through interfaces which reveal the functionality only as the only exposed portion of the ABB component.

See under : **5.2.2 Generic Characteristics**[20] : Very important points.

A Building Block's ... should be ...; i.e., ...

The way in which assets and capabilities are assembled ....

Every organization must ....

A good choice of ....

---

20. https://pubs.opengroup.org/togaf-standard/architecture-content/chap05.html#tag_05_02_02

Systems are built up ....

Wherever that is true, it is .....

Building Block is a favourite topic for Certification questions. You will come across many questions on this topic at different points of this courseware.

Read all about Building Block (ABB, SBB) Characteristics, if you are not clear about this questions and the correct answer.

Answer : C

———————————

Q 610 Which one of the following statements about TOGAF® Building Blocks is NOT true ?

A. They should not be reused in other enterprise architecture projects

B. They should have stable, published interfaces that allow other Building Block to interoperate with them

C. They are packages of functionality intended to meet the business needs across the organization

D. They have defined boundaries

Explanation :

Very idea of preparing Component Building Blocks during entire Architecture is to re-use them in other future projects to the extent possible. This is why Building Blocks are defined to be "**potentially re-usable**".

See **5.2.2 Generic Characteristics**[21] : Very important points.

▪ A building block is a .... defined to ... across an organization : Not just a single functionality, but a package. Components are always composed of smaller elements. So also a Building Block Component which combines many functional needs as its elemental architectural pieces.

▪ A building block has a ... that corresponds to the ... (such as ..., or ..) : 'Type' here means some identified portion, as per Content Metamodel. In other words it is ideally expected to be among one of the types shown in various figures in **TOGAF Content Framework and Enterprise Metamodel**[22]

Often TOGAF® is tailored to suit the Enterprise, and the metamodel is also tailored. This can be seen as green colored portions of **Figure 7-1: Overview of Architecture Repository**[23]. Study the examples given and then think of your own architectural experience where such types and examples have been used.

▪ A building block has a .... and is generally recognizable ..as "a thing" by .. experts : Clearly demarcated boundary so that one Building Block Component is distinguished from other. This is why we need a content metamodel definition for each 'type'.

---

21. https://pubs.opengroup.org/togaf-standard/architecture-content/chap05.html#tag_05_02_02

22. https://pubs.opengroup.org/togaf-standard/architecture-content/chap02.html

23. https://pubs.opengroup.org/togaf-standard/architecture-content/chap07.html#tagfcjh_16

▪ A building block may ....with other, ... building blocks : They are like Lego blocks. They are designed right from the beginning to be interoperable and interconnected in nature. Following characteristics explains how the Building Blocks become interconnected.

A good building block has the following characteristics :

— It considers ... and standards : Tending to be practical and closer to IT implementable reality.

— It may be ... building blocks : A Building Block Component may have different sub-Components. Like a Microservice Cluster is made up from many individual and re-usable services.

— It may be a ... building blocks : Even the granular Microservice mentioned above may have sub-assembled components of Application portion (the core service), data store (such as a Kafka topic) and infrastructure (like a docker image)

— Ideally a .. well specified : Thus we can arrive at, based on the example given in above two points, ideally and potentially re-usable services with API specifications. Any of them can be replaced by a equivalent service coded in another language or environment; any of them can be replaced with a better designed service, as long as the interface is not changed.

Get to know facts about Building Blocks. We should see them as ABB and SBB. Here, the term "Architecture" designates a description, and more precisely a logical view, as opposed to the "Solution," which represents a totally specified technically implementable reality.

Note clearly that an SBB is only an implementable reality. It is **NOT implemented** (coded and installed) **one** but is the architectural solution that is ready for implementation by the appropriate implementation agencies (PMO, Operations)

Answer : A

———————————

Q 611 Which of the following is about a deliverable is correct ?

A. It can be any artifact

B. It has to be a Solution Building Block

C. It cannot be catalog or a matrix

D. It is a work piece (work product) that describes an architecture from a specific viewpoint ?

E. It has to be a diagram

Explanation :

A deliverable is something mandated (specified by the EA to the Segment Architect as a contract of task to be completed).). See **Chapter 4. Architecture Deliverables**[24]

All other Answer Choices are incorrect as they distort the fact.

---

24. https://pubs.opengroup.org/togaf-standard/architecture-content/chap04.html

See under : **3.1 : Basic Concepts : Architectural Artifacts**[25]

In .... or ... the design of a system architecture, the ..., possibly using ..... An architecture view will ... of one or more ... chosen so as to demonstrate to a particular ... that their ... addressed in the ... architecture.

Answer Choice A) : Every artifact is not a deliverable. Only those which are specified to be produced as per a contractual work allocation. Other non-mandated outputs are additional artifacts, but not classified under 'deliverable'

Answer Choice B) : Solution Building Block or even Architecture Building Block can be a deliverable, depending on which Phase it is contractually specified (as a deliverable).

Answer Choice C) : **Not true that it cannot be catalog or a matrix.** It can be a catalog, matrix or a diagram.

Answer Choice E) : **Not true that it has to be a diagram.** It can be a catalog, matrix or a diagram.

Answer : D

Q 612 Which of the following statements is not correct ?

A. A view can be thought of as a template for a viewpoint

B. A viewpoint defines the perspective from which a view is taken

C. A viewpoint defines how to construct and use a view

D. A view is what a stakeholder sees

E. A view might describe business process for an IT system

Explanation :

A view can be thought of as a template for a viewpoint : **Not correct**, because, it is the other way round; a viewpoint is considered a template for a view.

See under **3.2.2 : Architecture View Creation Process**[26]

Generate views ... using ..

Following discussion is based on **3.4 Architecture Views and Architecture Viewpoints**[27]

Answer Choice B) : A viewpoint defines the perspective from which a view is taken : we can see that an architecture view can subset the system through the perspective of the stakeholder.

Answer Choice C) : A viewpoint defines how to construct and use a view : .. architecture view can be developed from the architecture viewpoint of the (pilot – standing for the stakeholder), which addresses the concerns.

---

25. https://pubs.opengroup.org/togaf-standard/architecture-content/chap03.html#tag_03_01

26. https://pubs.opengroup.org/togaf-standard/architecture-content/chap03.html#tag_03_02_02

27. https://pubs.opengroup.org/togaf-standard/architecture-content/chap03.html#tag_03_04

Answer Choice D) : A view is what a stakeholder sees : So, in essence, each architecture viewpoint is an abstract ... of how all the ..of a particular type view the system.

Answer Choice E) : A view might describe business process for an IT system : However, there are .. shared, such as .. and/or ....

Answer : A

———————

Q 613 Which of the following statements describing relationships between stakeholders, concerns, views, and viewpoints is correct ?

A. A concern is important to only one stakeholder

B. A stakeholder identifies one or more concerns

C. A viewpoint covers one concern

D. A viewpoint consists of one or more views

Explanation :

Answer Choices A) and C) should have been worded as one or more stakeholders / concerns.

Answer Choice D) is **incorrect**. Viewpoint address a concern which is related the view(s) of stakeholder(s). It does not contain them.

Who are stakeholders and why would they have one or more concerns ? Answer is found in : **3.1 Basic Concepts**[28]

"Stakeholders" are ...., having an interest in a system : Each one is important to be noted.

"Concerns" are ... relevant to .... Concerns may pertain to ..., including .. such as ... of the system : Note all of them again.

Taking points beyond this question but on same topic, we also note : Make a note all of them again. Quite important points.

An "architecture view" is ....

It consists of one or more ....

An "Architecture Model" is a ....

A model provides ....

In capturing or representing ..., the architect will typically create ....

An architecture view will ...

Also refer to **Figure 3-1 Basic Architectural Concepts**[29]

28. https://pubs.opengroup.org/togaf-standard/architecture-content/chap03.html#tag_03_01

29. https://pubs.opengroup.org/togaf-standard/architecture-content/chap03.html#tagfcjh_7

Answer : B

_____

Q 614 Which of the following does not apply to a Building Block ?

A. It is a package of functionality that meets business needs

B. It has published interfaces to access functionality

C. It may interoperate with other Building Blocks

D. It has a specification that is tightly coupled to its implementation

Explanation :

Building blocks should have a loose coupling to implementation to allow for multiple implementations and re-implementation. It is not meant to be tightly coupled.

See under : **5.2.2 Generic Characteristics**[30]

Read the explanation appearing under **Q 610**

A Building Block's ... should be loosely coupled to ...

And so on

Answer : D

_____

Q 615 Views and Viewpoints are used by an architect to capture or model the design of a system architecture. Which one of the following statements is true ?

A. A view is the perspective of an individual stakeholder

B. A viewpoint is the perspective of an individual stakeholder

C. Different stakeholders always share the same views

D. Different stakeholders always share the same viewpoints

Explanation :

A view is what you see; so it is connected with artifacts produced as an answering way to address a concern.

A viewpoint is where you are looking from – the vantage point or perspective that determines what you see. So it is connected with the concerns and issues of the stakeholders.

Diagrams or other Artifacts present the Architecture information (View) from a set of different perspectives (viewpoints) according to the requirements of the stakeholders.

---

30. https://pubs.opengroup.org/togaf-standard/architecture-content/chap05.html#tag_05_02_02

See : **3.1 Basic Concepts**[31]

A view is ..... A viewpoint is ... from – the .. point or ... that determines .... Diagrams or other Artifacts present the .... from a set of .. (viewpoints) according to the .. stakeholders.

An "architecture view" is a .... system.

An "Architecture Model" is a ... matter.

In capturing or representing ... using different tools.

▪ Architecture viewpoints are .. and can be ... for re-use; an architecture view is always ... for which it is created

▪ Every architecture view has an .... that describes it, at least implicitly : More important among the important ones.

In summary, then, ... are representations of the overall ... in terms .... stakeholders. They enable the ... their concerns.

Read the explanation appearing under **Q 613**

Answer : B

─────────────

Q 616 Which one of the following best describes the content of an Architecture Building Block ?

A. Defined implementation

B. Fundamental functionality

C. Products and components used to implement the functionality

D. Product or vendor-aware

E. Specific functionality

Explanation :

An ABB has fundamental functionality and attributes: semantic, unambiguous, including security capability and manageability.

We further see, in : **5.2.2 Generic Characteristics**[32]

Systems are built up from ...., so most ... have to ... with other .... Wherever that is true, it is important that ... are ... and reasonably .. : How are systems built ? What is said about interfaces here ?

Building blocks can be defined at ..., depending on what ... has been reached. For instance, ... description. Later on, a ... may be decomposed into ... and may be accompanied by a ... : What is said about decomposition here ?

The level of detail to ...value (for example, ...specification).

Looking into : **5.2.3.1 Characteristics**[33] and **5.2.3.2 Specification Content**[34] : Important to be take note of.

---

31. https://pubs.opengroup.org/togaf-standard/architecture-content/chap03.html#tag_03_01

32. https://pubs.opengroup.org/togaf-standard/architecture-content/chap05.html#tag_05_02_02

ABBs :

▪ Capture ..

▪ Direct and guide ...

ABB specifications .. as a minimum :

▪ Fundamental ..

▪ Interfaces: ..

▪ ... with other Building Blocks

▪ ... with required ..

▪ Map to ...

Do go through explanation appearing under **Q 608**

Answer : B

───────────

Q 617 Which of the following statements on TOGAF® Building Blocks is true ?

A. A good Building Block should not be composed of other Building Blocks

B. Architecture Building Blocks should be first selected in Phase D

C. Building Block specifications should be loosely coupled to implementation

D. Custom developments are known as Architecture Building Blocks

Explanation :

Building Block specifications should be loosely coupled to implementation. Other three Answer Choices indicate **incorrect facts**.

See under : **5.2.2 Generic Characteristics**[35]

A Building Block's ...

The way in which ...

▪ ... is a package of functionality ..

▪ ...has a type ...

▪ ... has a defined ...

───────────

33. https://pubs.opengroup.org/togaf-standard/architecture-content/chap05.html#tag_05_02_03_01

34. https://pubs.opengroup.org/togaf-standard/architecture-content/chap05.html#tag_05_02_03_02

35. https://pubs.opengroup.org/togaf-standard/architecture-content/chap05.html#tag_05_02_02

▪ ... may interoperate with ..

A good Building Block has the following characteristics :

— It considers ..

— It may be assembled ...

— It may be a subassembly of ...

— ... re-usable and replaceable, and well specified

Read the detailed explanation appearing under **Q 610**

Answer : C

Q 618 Which of the following applies to an Architecture Building Block ?

A. It defines the functionality to be implemented

B. It defines the implementation

C. It defines what products and components will implement the functionality

D. It is product or vendor-aware

Explanation :

ABBs define functionality – not implementation.

Looking into : **5.2.3.1 Characteristics**[36] and **5.2.3.2 Specification Content**[37]

Read explanation appearing under **Q 616**

Answer : A

Q 619 Which one of the following statements about Viewpoints is correct ?

A. A Viewpoint is always specific to an architecture

B. A Viewpoint is used to create views in Phases E and F

C. A Viewpoint is used as a template to create a view

D. A Viewpoint is what a stakeholder sees

Explanation :

---

36. https://pubs.opengroup.org/togaf-standard/architecture-content/chap05.html#tag_05_02_03_01

37. https://pubs.opengroup.org/togaf-standard/architecture-content/chap05.html#tag_05_02_03_02

A Viewpoint, something that an Architect has to consider while looking at the point of view of the Stakeholder (and their concerns) is combination and collection of requisite Patterns, Templates, and other conventions. This needed for constructing each type of **View** each type of artifact Building Block.

Thus, a Viewpoint focusses the perspective of the Architect, narrowing down **for each participant**.

The end result of such a focus is the creation of number of views of the architecture – Building Blocks.

We also know that these are in the form of catalogues, matrices, diagrams, documents, or other document elements.

Answer Choice A) : A Viewpoint is always specific to an architecture : **Not tru**e, because, we see in **3.1 Basic Concepts**[38] as :

An "architecture viewpoint" is a specification of the ...

Answer Choice B) : A Viewpoint is used to create views in Phases E and F : **Not true**, since views are created in all phases of ADM and all the more in Phases B, C, D.

Answer Choice D) : A Viewpoint is what a stakeholder sees : **Not true**, because, we see in **3.1 Basic Concepts**[39] as :

An architecture view is ...

Viewpoint and View are also favourite question focus points.

Answer : C

Q 620 Which of the following statements is not correct ?

A. A concern might include performance and reliability

B. A concern is an area of interest

C. Concerns are key interests of the stakeholders

D. Concern and requirement are synonymous

Explanation :

They are not synonymous as concerns are used to derive requirements.

See under : **3.1 Basic Concepts**[40]

The terms "concern" and "requirement" are not synonymous. A concern always is an area of interest to someone. Here it is the area of issue or idea relevant to the stakeholder. So, system reliability or System performance are all could happen to be a concern / area of interest for some stakeholders.

---

38. https://pubs.opengroup.org/togaf-standard/architecture-content/chap03.html#tag_03_01

39. https://pubs.opengroup.org/togaf-standard/architecture-content/chap03.html#tag_03_01

40. https://pubs.opengroup.org/togaf-standard/architecture-content/chap03.html#tag_03_01

The reason why architects should identify concerns and associate them with architecture viewpoints, is to ensure that those concerns will be addressed in some fashion by the models of the architecture.

For example, if the only architecture viewpoint selected by an architect is a structural architecture viewpoint, then reliability concerns are almost certainly not being addressed, since they cannot be represented in a structural model. Within that concern, stakeholders may have many distinct requirements : different classes of users may have very different reliability requirements for different capabilities of the system.

We further look into **3.1 Basic Concepts**[41] for confirming correctness of other answer choices

Answer choice A) : A concern might include performance and reliability is **correct** : Concerns may pertain to any aspect of the ..., ..., ..., including considerations such .... and may determine the ... of the system.

Answer choice B) : A concern is an area of interest is **correct** : "Concerns" are ....some stakeholders.

Answer choice C) : Concerns are key interests of the stakeholders is **correct** : "Stakeholders" are ... a system.

Answer : D

————————————

Q 621 Stakeholders and their concerns are key concepts in TOGAF®. Which one of the following statements is false ?

A. Concerns are key interests that are crucially important to stakeholders

B. Concerns should be SMART and have specific metrics

C. Stakeholders can be individuals, teams, or organizations

D. Stakeholders have key roles in, or concerns about, the system

Explanation :

See under : **3.1 Basic Concepts**[42]

"Concerns" are the key interests that are crucially important to the stakeholders in the system and determine the acceptability of the system.

Concerns may pertain to ....evolvability ,,,.

The terms "concern" and "requirement" are not synonymous. Concerns are the root of the process of decomposition into requirements. Concerns are represented in the architecture by these requirements. Requirements should be SMART (e.g., specific metrics).

Incidentally, SMART stands as : An acronym for Specific, Measurable, Actionable, Realistic, and Time-bound

This is an approach to ensure that targets and objectives are set in a way that can be achieved and subjected to measurement.

We also pick from the[43] Series Guide on : Business Scenarios, as :

Specific, by defining what needs to be done in the business

Measurable, through clear metrics for success

Actionable, by :

— Clearly segmenting the problem

— Providing the basis for determining elements and plans for the solution

Realistic, in that the problem can be solved within the bounds of physical reality, time, and cost constraints

Time-bound, in that there is a clear statement of when the solution opportunity expires

Answer : B

———————

Q 622 Gap analysis is a key step in validating the architecture in Phase B : Business Architecture. Which one of the following statements is true ?

A. Gap analysis highlights services that are available

B. Gap analysis highlights the impacts of change

C. Gap analysis highlights services that are yet to be procured or prepared

D. Gap analysis identifies areas where the Data Architecture needs to change

E. Gap analysis can be used to resolve conflicts amongst different viewpoints

Explanation :

Gap analysis, apart from looking (and solving for) many types of gaps, also includes highlighting and focussing on services that are yet to be procured or prepared.

A key step in validating an architecture is to consider what may have been forgotten or what is yet to be prepared / procured.

See : **5.1 Introduction**[44] : Gap Analysis : ADM Techniques portion of TOGAF® Standard Fundamental Content Version 10

A key step in ... is to consider what may have ....

The architecture must support .... The most critical source of .... considered is stakeholder ...

Potential sources of gaps include : Get to know these and all other types of Gaps mentioned in this Chapter.

▪ Business domain gaps:

— ...gaps ... — ...gaps ... — ... gaps ...

— ...gaps — ...gaps — ...gaps — ... gaps ...

The preamble above this section also reads as : The technique known as ... is widely used in the .... to ... is being developed. The basic ...a shortfall between the ..; that is, items that have been ..... : Used exhaustively while carrying out the ADM process. While the Architect will 'perform' Gap Analysis by looking inti missing items, to-be-filled-items and to-be-removed items of artifact Building Blocks, the Senior Architect may validate the work done by looking against from a Gap between Baseline and Target.

Answer : C

———————

Q 623 Which of the following is defined by TOGAF® as a representation of a system from the perspective of a related set of concerns ?

A. Architecture Building Block

B. Capability Architecture

C. Statement of Work

D. View

E. Viewpoint

Explanation :

View is a representation of a system from the perspective of a related set of concerns.

See under : **3.1 Basic Concepts**[45]

An "architecture view" is .... It consists of ... .

View is a representation of a ...

On incorrect answer choices :

Answer Choice A) : Architecture Building Block : This does not represent a system from the perspective of a related set of concerns. This is actual units of representations of architectural work done.

Answer Choice B) : Capability Architecture : Not something to do with concerns. We see from **7.2 Architecture Landscape**[46] under Architecture Content part of TOGAF® Standard Fundamental Content Version 10

Capability Architectures[47] show in a more detailed fashion how the enterprise can support a particular unit of capability.

---

45. https://pubs.opengroup.org/togaf-standard/architecture-content/chap03.html#tag_03_01

46. https://pubs.opengroup.org/togaf-standard/architecture-content/chap07.html#tag_07_02

47. https://pubs.opengroup.org/togaf-standard/applying-the-adm/chap04.html#tagfcjh_8

Capability Architectures are used to provide an overview of ...., ..., and ... increments and allow for individual ... and ... to be grouped within ... and .... : A way to check how progress is made in Capability Enhancement of the business and architectural portions of the Enterprise. Work Packages, as prepared in Phase E will contain incremental Capability in the form of Transition Architectures that can be built over current Capability.

Take a Business Capability, in easy to understand terms as : Current : Manually recording items sold. Target : Automated recording of sales in real time. Incremental Steps : Bring in Point Of Sale (like Bar Code or QR code). Introduce them for some fast moving items first and incrementally for all items.

Sense these items though hardware readers and software integration for both billing and inventory work (Two Capabilities incremented : Automated billing and automated sales recording). And so on till the automation process is complete. Note that the Business Capabilities here are achieved through IT enablement.

Answer Choice C) : Statement of Work comes up even before concerns about specific project areas are observed. See : **4.2.20 Statement of Architecture Work**[48] : 4. Architecture Deliverables under Architecture Content part of TOGAF® Standard Fundamental Content Version 10

This .... that will be used to complete an .... cycle. The Statement of Architecture Work is typically the ... successful execution of the architecture project will be ...and may form the ... between the ... services.

Answer Choice E) : Viewpoint : is a collection of Patterns, Templates, and conventions for constructing one type of **View.**

Answer : D

Q 624 According to TOGAF®, which of the following terms is defined as the key interests that are crucially important to stakeholders ?

A. Concerns

B. Principles

C. Requirements

D. Views

E. Viewpoints

Explanation :

Concerns are interests that are crucially important to stakeholders. Concerns come from stakeholders and Architect is expected to address them.

See under : **3.1 Basic Concepts**[49]

"Concerns" are ...

---

48. https://pubs.opengroup.org/togaf-standard/architecture-content/chap04.html#tag_04_02_20

49. https://pubs.opengroup.org/togaf-standard/architecture-content/chap03.html#tag_03_01

Concerns may pertain to ....

Typically, it is the +preparation for business transformation needs or for radical infrastructure changes that initiates an Enterprise Architecture review or development.

Also see under : **1.1 Executive Overview**[50] : **What specifically would prompt the development of an Enterprise Architecture ?**[51] : under Introduction and Core Concepts part of TOGAF® Standard Fundamental Content Version 10

Often key people ... for new .... Such people are commonly referred to as the "... in the change : Enterprise Architecture action is called for when Business Transformation is necessity. Such a need for change is identified by the Stakeholders.

The role of the architect is to address their concerns by :

▪ Identifying and ... that the ... have : Take notice of (identify) and take it further as Requirements which needs an implementable solution (refining).

▪ Developing views of the architecture that show .... to be addressed : Produce Building Block Views, through due process.

▪ Showing the ...that are going to be made in ... of ... : Look into conflicting area of concerns and arrive at a trade-off path that has evaluated all possible alternatives.

Without the Enterprise Architecture, it is .... that all the concerns and requirements will be .... : Thus Enterprise Architecture is the only way to take the concerns and make them as Requirements first and Solutions next.

Answer : A

––––––––––––––––

Q 625 Which of the following does TOGAF® describe as package of functionality defined to meet business needs across an organization ?

A. An application

B. An architecture viewpoint

C. A Building Block

D. A deliverable

E. A solution architecture

Explanation :

A Building block (especially an ABB) is a package of functionality defined to meet business needs across an organization.

See under : **5.2.2 Generic Characteristics**[52]

---

50. https://pubs.opengroup.org/togaf-standard/introduction/chap01.html#tag_01_01

51. https://pubs.opengroup.org/togaf-standard/introduction/chap01.html#tag_01_01_00_04

Read the explanation appearing under **Q 610**

Answer : C

Q 626 Which of the following is used to create architecture models addressing stakeholder concerns ?

A. Catalog

B. Matrix

C. Diagram

D. View

E. Viewpoint

Explanation :

View is used to create architecture models (Artifact Building Blocks and other documents) which in turn addresses the stakeholder concerns.

See under : **3.2 Developing Architecture Views in the ADM**[53] :

The choice of which particular .... to develop is one of the key decisions that the architect has to make. The architect has a ...., in terms of ... so doing (as between .., for example) : What is the key decision to be made ? Decision will be based on what ?

Under **3.4.1 Example of Architecture Views and Architecture Viewpoints**[54] : Example used says :

One architecture view can be ...

Example used says : One architecture view can be developed from the architecture viewpoint of the pilot, which addresses the pilot's concerns. An architecture viewpoint is a model (or description) of the information contained in a view.

On incorrect answer choices :

Answer Choice A) Catalog : A structured list of architectural outputs of a similar kind, used for reference. So, it cannot be, by itself be used to create architecture models addressing stakeholder concerns. It can be useful in a View.

Answer Choice B) Matrix : A format for showing the relationship between two (or more) architectural elements in a grid format. So, it cannot be, by itself be used to create architecture models addressing stakeholder concerns. It can be useful in a View.

---

52. https://pubs.opengroup.org/togaf-standard/architecture-content/chap05.html#tag_05_02_02

53. https://pubs.opengroup.org/togaf-standard/architecture-content/chap03.html#tag_03_02

54. https://pubs.opengroup.org/togaf-standard/architecture-content/chap03.html#tag_03_04_01

Answer Choice C) Diagram : Every diagram is drawn as per its content and notations as prescribed. it cannot be, by itself be used to create architecture models addressing stakeholder concerns. It can be useful in a View, especially through a modelling process.

Answer Choice E) Viewpoint : is a collection of Patterns, Templates, and conventions for constructing one type of **View**. So, it cannot be, by itself be used to create architecture models addressing stakeholder concerns.

Answer : D

———————

Q 627 Which of the following relationship between view, viewpoint and architecture is correct ?

A. View can also be called the definition or schema for that kind of architecture Viewpoint

B. An "architecture viewpoint" is a specification of the conventions for a particular kind of architecture view

C. A "Model " establishes conventions for a type of "Model kind"

D. An architecture View references one or more model kinds

E. An architecture Viewpoint incorporates one or more models

Explanation :

Only answer Choice B) is correct, as per TOGAF® explanation about View and Viewpoints.

All other Answer Choices give **wrong points** about View, Viewpoints, Model, and Model kind

See : **3.1 Basic Concepts**[55]

An "architecture viewpoint" is a ... view. It establishes the conventions for .. a system-of-interest : A vantage viewing point (from Stakeholder perspective), suggesting the way to address the concerns. All View creation steps start from one point-of-view (Viewpoint) or other.

A "Model Kind" establishes ... modeling : The thought process before actual modelling starts. Guides on the kind of model (which all Catalog s/ Matrices / Diagrams to be chosen).

An architecture viewpoint ... one or more models : Thus Viewpoints happen to be crucial guiding references in choosing the model and the View which are the spirit behind g the artifacts.

An architecture view will ... of the system architecture : Ultimate result is what Architect produces as View – the Building Blocks along with all

Answer : B

---

55. https://pubs.opengroup.org/togaf-standard/architecture-content/chap03.html#tag_03_01

Q 628 Not a benefit of View Creation Process

A. Advantages of creating the required views by referring to library, selecting the viewpoints and generating the views

B. Reducing tasks for the architects

C. Offering better comprehensibility for stakeholders

D. Enhancing confidence in the validity of the views

Explanation :

Main thing to note is that 'View Creation Process' is nothing but the steps taken in any of the Phases B to D. The ultimate result of each these Phases is that View (Building Blocks deliverables and supporting documents.) are produced, peer validated (Resolve impact across Architectural Landscape), Stakeholder approved (Conduct Formal Stakeholder Review) and so on.

Answer Choice A) is not among the benefit of View Creation process as given in TOGAF® documentation.

See Section : **3.2.2 : Architecture View Creation Process**[56]

This approach .. following benefits :

▪ Less work for the ...

▪ Better comprehensibility for ...

▪ Greater confidence in the ...

Also see in same link as above :

Create the ... for a particular architecture by following these steps : **(Immediately look for steps in Phases B to D right now and compare these)**

1. Refer to .. viewpoints

2. Select ..viewpoints (based on the .. by views)

3. Generate .. as templates

Answer : A

Q 629 Architectural Concern will not pertain to

A. Affordability

B. Performance

C. Reliability

---

56. https://pubs.opengroup.org/togaf-standard/architecture-content/chap03.html#tag_03_02_02

D. Distribution

E. Security

F. Evolvability

Explanation :

Affordability is not a concern of Architecture. It is a financial concern.

Concern[57] : An interest in a system ....

Note : Concerns .... of the system.

We see this in **3.1 Basic Concepts**[58]

"Concerns" are ... system's ..., including considerations such as ...

Also See : **3.2 Developing Architecture Views in the ADM**[59]

The typical progression is from ... using a technique such as ... to properly identify ...; and from ..., continually referring ..

Answer : A

———————

Q 630 One that does not apply to the term : Viewpoint

A. Specification of the conventions for a particular kind of architecture view

B. Definition or schema for that kind of architecture view

C. Establishes conventions for a type of modelling

D. Incorporates one or more models

Explanation :

A View incorporates one or more models; not the Viewpoint.

See : **3.1 Basic Concepts**[60] :

Also see : **4.21 Architecture Viewpoint**[61]

An "architecture viewpoint" is ... view.

It can also be called the ....

---

57. https://pubs.opengroup.org/togaf-standard/introduction/chap04.html#tag_04_37

58. https://pubs.opengroup.org/togaf-standard/architecture-content/chap03.html#tag_03_01

59. https://pubs.opengroup.org/togaf-standard/architecture-content/chap03.html#tag_03_02

60. https://pubs.opengroup.org/togaf-standard/architecture-content/chap03.html#tag_03_01

61. https://pubs.opengroup.org/togaf-standard/introduction/chap04.html#tag_04_21

It establishes the ... to address a specific concern ... about a ...

A "Model Kind" establishes ....

An architecture viewpoint ...; an architecture view ....

Do go through explanation appearing under **Q 627**

Also refer to **Figure 3-1 Basic Architectural Concepts**[62] and infer the various relationships, especially between :

Architecture Viewpoint -> governs : Architecture View

Architecture View <> contained in : Architecture Description

Architecture Description-> expresses : Architecture

Model Kind -> governs : Architecture Model

Model Kind <> contained in : Architecture Viewpoint

Architecture Viewpoint -> frames : Concern

Stakeholder -> has : Concern

Stakeholder -> has interests in : System-of-Interest (our project portfolio)

Note : 'contained in' means, part of.

Answer : D

––––––––––––––––

Q 631 Complete the sentence. In TOGAF®, legacy systems and processes that are going to be used again in the future are considered _____

A. Architecture Building Blocks

B. Components

C. Patterns

D. Re-usable Building Blocks

E. Solution Building Blocks

Explanation :

Anything of architectural nature and has a potential to be used at least once again is a Re-usable Building Block. Architectural ideas (ABBs) and process descriptions from legacy applications also fit in this.

We also know from **1.1 Overview**[63] : 1. Introduction under Architecture Content part of TOGAF® Standard Fundamental Content Version 10 that :

---

62. https://pubs.opengroup.org/togaf-standard/architecture-content/chap03.html#tagfcjh_7

▪ A **Building Block** represents .....

The Architecture Content Framework ... three categories to ... :

▪ A **deliverable** is a ....

So, deliverable for current project may be based on what was there in the legacy architecture.

.▪ An **artifact** is an ...

Artifacts are generally classified as ...

So, artifacts to be prepared on legacy ideas duly improvised for current requirement and present level of architectural advancements.

▪ A **Building Block** represents a ...

So, artifacts duly combined herein as Building block components would have re-used the legacy Blocks suitably.

Answer : D

———————

Q 632 Which are the three main categories of architectural work product that Architecture Content Framework specifies ?

A. Architecture Vision, Architecture Requirements Specification and Architecture Roadmap

B. Source Architecture, Target Architecture and Gap Analysis

C. Architecture Vision, Architecture Design Document and Transition Architecture

D. Building Block, Artifact and Deliverable

E. Request for Architecture Work, Statement of Architecture Work and Architecture Contract

Explanation :

TOGAF® mentions very clearly that Building Block, Artifact and Deliverable are the three work products. This is specified in the Architecture Content Framework with more details about each.

See under : **3.6 Deliverables, Artifacts, and Building Blocks**[64] under Introduction and Core Concepts part of TOGAF® Standard Fundamental Content Version 10

Also from : **1.1 Overview**[65] : 1. Introduction under Architecture Content part of TOGAF® Standard Fundamental Content Version 10

The Architecture Content Framework ... to describe the type of architectural work product within the context of use :

63. https://pubs.opengroup.org/togaf-standard/architecture-content/chap01.html#tag_01_01

64. https://pubs.opengroup.org/togaf-standard/introduction/chap03.html#tag_03_06

65. https://pubs.opengroup.org/togaf-standard/architecture-content/chap01.html#tag_01_01

- A **deliverable** is a ...

- An **artifact** is an ....

- A **Building Block** represents ...

Answer : D

Q 633 Which portion of the TOGAF® document provides a structural model for architectural content that allows the major work products that an architect creates to be consistently defined, structured, and presented

A. Introduction and Core Concepts portion of TOGAF® Standard Fundamental Content Version 10

B. ADM Techniques portion of TOGAF® Standard Fundamental Content Version 10

C. ADM Techniques portion of TOGAF® Standard Fundamental Content Version 10

D. Architecture Content portion of TOGAF® Standard Fundamental Content Version 10

Explanation :

A study of each free-standing document part (Portions) of TOGAF® documentation reveals that Architecture Content part deals with this.

See under : **3.6 Deliverables, Artifacts, and Building Blocks**[66] under Introduction and Core Concepts part of TOGAF® Standard Fundamental Content Version 10

The TOGAF® Architecture Content section provides a structural model for architectural content that allows major work products to be consistently defined, structured, and presented.

Other parts of TOGAF® not appearing in above Answer Choices, just for information are :

Applying the ADM part of TOGAF® Standard Fundamental Content Version 10

Enterprise Architecture Capability and Governance part of TOGAF® Standard Fundamental Content Version 10

See : Architecture Content part of TOGAF® Standard Fundamental Content Version 10[67] and **1.1 Overview**[68]

Architects executing the Architecture Development Method (ADM) will produce ...

The content framework provides ... structured, and presented.

The content framework provided ... to be used as a stand-alone framework for ...

On incorrect answer choices :

---

66. https://pubs.opengroup.org/togaf-standard/introduction/chap03.html#tag_03_06

67. https://pubs.opengroup.org/togaf-standard/architecture-content/index.html

68. https://pubs.opengroup.org/togaf-standard/architecture-content/chap01.html#tag_01

Answer Choice A) : ADM Techniques[69] : This part contains a collection of guidelines and techniques available for use in applying the ADM.

Answer Choice B) : Enterprise Architecture Capability and Governance[70] : This part discusses the organization, processes, skills, roles, and responsibilities required to establish and operate an architecture practice within an enterprise.

Answer Choice D) : Architecture Governance Framework : This Framework is described within Architecture Capability Framework and is part of what is given in the link above.

Answer Choice E) : TOGAF® Reference Models : This is one among the few refence model mentioned in certain ADM phases.

For details refer to Series Guides in TOGAF® Library, which are not part of Certification syllabus.

Do go through the explanation appearing under **Q 633**

Answer : C

---

69. https://pubs.opengroup.org/togaf-standard/adm-techniques/index.html

70. https://pubs.opengroup.org/togaf-standard/ea-capability-and-governance/index.html

Non-conventional Multiple choice questions start from here. Go through them with attention since such questions are hallmark of TOGAF® 10 Exam

Q 650

Consider the following partial descriptions :

1 ... should be loosely coupled to its implementation; i.e., it should be possible to realize a building block in several different ways without impacting the boundary or specification of the building block

2 ... is dependent on the objectives of the architecture and, in some cases, less detail may be of greater value (for example, when presenting the capabilities of an enterprise, a single clear and concise picture has more value than a dense 100-page specification)

3 ... can lead to improvements in legacy system integration, interoperability, and flexibility in the creation of new systems and applications

4 ... so most building blocks have to interoperate with other building blocks. Wherever that is true, it is important that the interfaces to a building block are published and reasonably stable

Which phrases of terminologies match and complete these descriptions ?

- A. 1 A building block's boundary and specification 2 A good choice of building blocks 3 The level of detail to which a building block should be specified 4 Systems are built up from collections of building blocks
- B. 1 A building block's boundary and specification 2 A good choice of building blocks 3 Systems are built up from collections of building blocks 4 The level of detail to which a building block should be specified
- C. 1 Systems are built up from collections of building blocks, 2 The level of detail to which a building block should be specified 3 A good choice of building blocks 4 A building block's boundary and specification
- D. 1 A building block's boundary and specification 2 The level of detail to which a building block should be specified is 3 A good choice of building blocks 4 Systems are built up from collections of building blocks

Explanation :

See : **5.2.2 Generic Characteristics**[71] : 5. Building Blocks under Architecture Content part of TOGAF® Standard Fundamental Content Version 10

1 ... should be loosely coupled to ...; i.e., it should be possible to .... building block

2 The level of detail to ... is dependent on the ... and, in some cases, less ... (for example, ...)

3 A good choice of ... can lead to ..., and flexibility in ....

4 Systems are built up from ..., so most building blocks ... with ....

Wherever ..., it is important that ... stable

Answer : D

---

71. https://pubs.opengroup.org/togaf-standard/architecture-content/chap05.html#tag_05_02

Q 651

Read the table below and spot the row that has wrong statement(s) in it :

Row	
A	The process of building block definition takes place gradually as the ADM is followed, mainly in Phases A, B, C, and D. It is an evolutionary and iterative process because as definition proceeds, detailed information about the functionality required, the constraints imposed on the architecture, and the availability of products may affect the choice and the content of building blocks. The selected set of ABBs is then refined in an iterative process to arrive at a set of SBBs which can either be bought off-the-shelf or custom developed
B	The process of building block definition takes place gradually as the ADM is followed, mainly in Phases B, C, and D. It is an evolutionary and iterative process because as definition proceeds, detailed information about the functionality required, the constraints imposed on the architecture, and the availability of products may affect the choice and the content of building blocks. The major work in these steps consists of identifying the ABBs required to meet the business goals and objectives.
C	The process of building block definition takes place gradually as the ADM is followed, mainly in Phases A, B, C, and D. It is an evolutionary and iterative process because as definition proceeds, detailed information about the functionality required, the constraints imposed on the architecture, and the availability of products may affect the choice and the content of building blocks. The major work in these steps consists of identifying the ABBs required to meet the business goals and objectives.
D	The major work in these steps consists of identifying the ABBs required to meet the business goals and objectives. The selected set of ABBs is then refined in an iterative process to arrive at a set of SBBs which can either be bought off-the-shelf or custom developed.

Explanation :

See : **5.3.2 Building Block Specification Process in the ADM**[72]

The process of building block definition ... as the ..., mainly in **Phases A, B, C, and D**.

It is an ... process because as .., detailed .., the ..., and the ... may affect the ....

Answer : B

Q 652

Look at the following illustration :

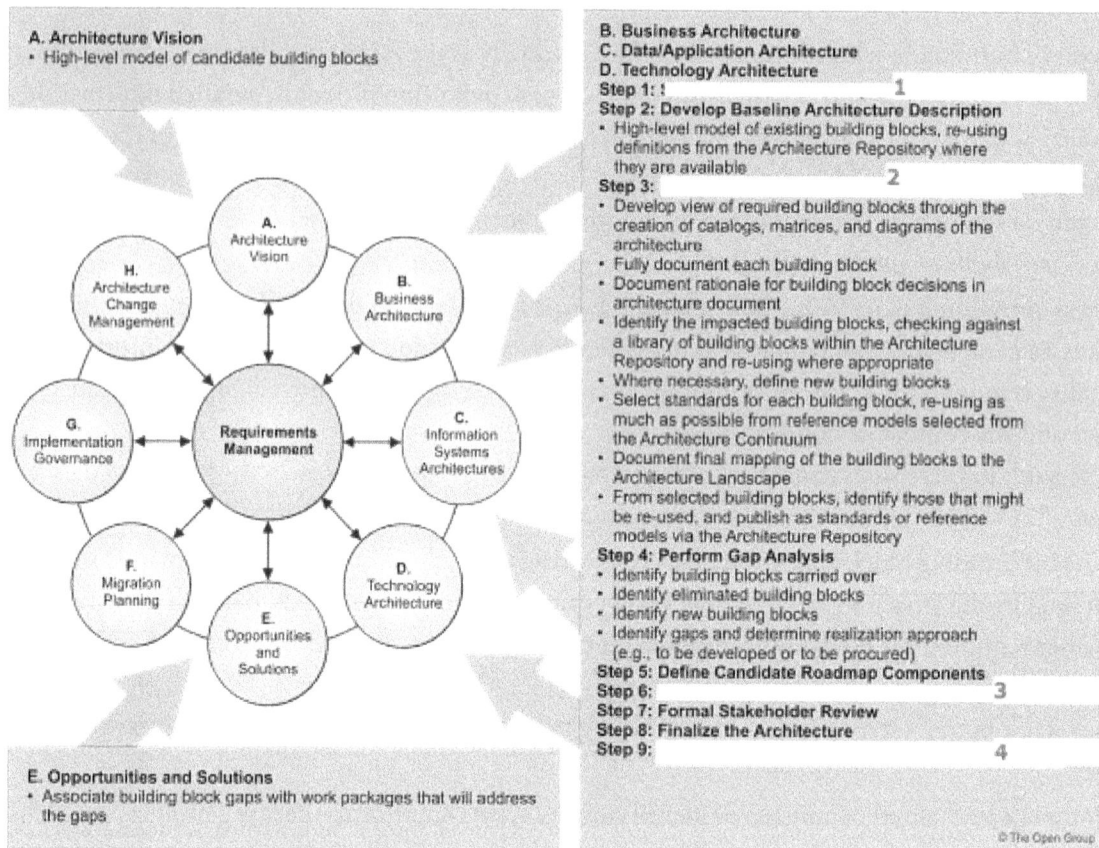

IDENTIFY THE RIGHT combination of the **1 2 3 4** marked steps that are missing in the image :

A. 1. Select reference models, viewpoints, and tools 2. Develop Target Business Architecture Description 3. Resolve impacts across the Architecture Landscape 4. Create/Update the Architecture Definition Document

B. 1. Select reference models, viewpoints, and tools 2. Develop Target Technology Architecture Description 3. Resolve impacts across the Architecture Landscape 4. Create/Update the Architecture Definition Document

C. 1. Select reference models, viewpoints, and tools 2. Resolve impacts across the Architecture Landscape 3. Develop Target Business Architecture Description 4. Create/Update the Architecture Definition Document

D. 1. Select reference models, viewpoints, and tools 2. Resolve impacts across the Architecture Landscape 3. Create/Update the Architecture Definition Document 4. Develop Target Technology Architecture Description

Explanation :

Look into : **Figure 5-1: Key ADM Phases/Steps at which Building Blocks are Evolved/Specified**[73]

Note that this illustration is regarding Phase D : Technology Architecture

Answer : B

73. https://pubs.opengroup.org/togaf-standard/architecture-content/Figures/37_bb_evolution.png

Looking at Official Level 1 Syllabus of Unit 7 – Architecture Content

Remembering Level Expected, through definitions, list of things involved or basic description of

TOGAF® Standard deliverables created and consumed in different TOGAF® ADM phases (covered under respective phases to some extent and is consolidated here as) :

Architecture Contract

Architecture Definition Document

Architecture Principles

Architecture Requirements Specification

Architecture Roadmap

Architecture Vision

Business Principles, Business Goals, and Business Drivers

Capability Assessment

Change Request

Communications Plan

Compliance Assessment

Implementation and Migration Plan

Implementation Governance Model

Request for Architecture Work

Requirements Impact Assessment

Statement of Architecture Work

UNDERSTANDING LEVEL of due explanation and summarization is expected in the following :

Define and explain the following key concepts : stakeholders, concerns, architecture views, architecture viewpoints, and their relationships.

Explain what building blocks are and their use in the ADM

Module 7 : Phase C : Application Architecture portion of Information Systems Architecture

———

Some questions on Phase C as a whole and not on Application Architecture may also feature in here.

Note that questions do come up with answer choices and correct answer picked up from other modules beyond these. Revisit all questions after revising the whole of TOGAF®. This particular module may attract very few Level 1 questions. The reason is that most of the Application Architecture techniques may have technology platform and brand specific platforms like languages, library APIs, development tool specific issues etc., Since TOGAF® is neutral to all these, questions on such specifics will be avoided.

Cross References shown as 'See' herein refer to the **7. Phase C : Information Systems Architectures — Application Architecture**[1] under Architecture Development Method part of TOGAF® Standard Fundamental Content Version 10

In case any other free-standing document of TOGAF® Standard Fundamental Content Version 10 or Series Guide is referenced, that is explicitly mentioned.

Q 701 In Phase C, Information Systems Architectures, which one of the following describes a top-down design and bottom-up implementation approach ?

A. Architecture development in both domains is done concurrently

B. Design and implementation are executed in reverse order

C. Design is centred on the development of the Technology Architecture

D. When the design work is completed, implementation work proceeds starting with the Technology domain

E. The architecture design work is re-factored frequently to facilitate alignment with the existing technology infrastructure

Explanation :

One common implementation approach is top-down design and bottom-up implementation, where design work is undertaken through the four architecture domains (Business, Data or Application, Application or Data, Technology), and when completed then implementation occurs in reverse domain order (Technology .... Business). But this point in Answer Choice B) is not the focus of this question.

This question is appearing in most mock examinations. But what is available in TOGAF® documentation is only about : See : **5.2 Approach**[2] : 5. Phase C: Information Systems Architectures under Architecture Development Method part of TOGAF® Standard Fundamental Content Version 10

Prepare yourself for another possible question with the following.

---

1. https://pubs.opengroup.org/togaf-standard/adm/chap07.html

2. https://pubs.opengroup.org/togaf-standard/adm/chap05.html#tag_05_02

Phase C involves some .... of ... and ... Architecture, **in either order.**

Advocates exist for .... For example, ... recommends a data-driven approach.

On the other hand, ... — such as those for ...Planning (...), ... Management (C...), etc. — often provide a combination of ... and ... logic, and some organizations take an ...., whereby they recognize certain .. as forming the core ..., and take the ... of those .... as the ... of architecture effort (the integration issues ... challenge) : Note the examples of Packaged solutions where Application Architecture work may precede Data Architecture work.

This position reveals, in crystal clear terms that whole Phase C involves some combination of Data and Application Architecture, the order of which comes first is not important. It depends on the situation and TOGAF® does not stipulate whether Data Architectures comes before Application Architecture or vice versa.

Nevertheless the section indicates certain major application systems (ERP and CRM are quoted here; it can be anything other than such a packed solution also) where an application-driven approach is preferred. These are situations where core applications become the focus of architecture effort with challenges coming up from integration angle.

Answer : D

Q 702 Which of the following documents acts as the deliverable container for the Business, Data, Application, and Technology architectural artifacts ?

A. Architecture Contract

B. Architecture Definition Document

C. Architecture Requirements Specification

D. Architecture Roadmap

E. Architecture Vision

Explanation :

"Deliverable Container" : Means the artifacts are placed in certain other repository but this Document contains just references (links) to them, But details below shows how other details are also form part of this Architecture Definition Document. This is the deliverable container for the core architectural artifacts created during a project. This document is initiated (probably empty or sketchy) in Phase A but has relevance in most subsequent Phases. Since more than one portfolio will be going through its own iteration within ADM at a given time, the Architecture Definition Document and its comparison Architecture Requirements Specification will have to prepared one each per portfolio.

4.2.3 Architecture Definition Document[3] : Purpose : under 4.2 Deliverable Descriptions[4] : 4. Architecture Deliverables under Architecture Content part of TOGAF® Standard Fundamental Content Version 10

Purpose : The Architecture Definition Document spans ....domains (.., ..., ..., and ...) and also examines ....states of the ...(...., ..., and ....) : Spans over what ? Examines what ? Note the three states.

---

3. https://pubs.opengroup.org/togaf-standard/architecture-content/chap04.html#tag_04_02_03

4. https://pubs.opengroup.org/togaf-standard/architecture-content/chap04.html#tag_04_02

The .... is a companion to the ..., with a complementary objective : ▪ The ... provides a ... of the solution and aims to communicate the intent of the architects ▪ The .... provides a ... of the solution, stating .... that must be met during the ...of the architecture : Which is companion to what ? What are the complementary objectives ? Which provides what kind of view ?

Note the entire contents : All are important. Also note that Phase A : Architecture Vision has started with these details, at an outline level.

▪ Scope : The scope enveloping the portfolio.

▪ Goals, ... : What are we aiming at and what could be the stumbling blocks ?

▪ Architecture ... : Which Principles as defined in Preliminary Phase are to be followed in the work of this portfolio.

▪ .... Architecture : The take-off point.

▪ Architecture ... (for ...to be...) : — ... models — ... models — ... models — ... models : Focus in on which one or more of these domains ?

▪ .... for architectural approach : The justification, as prepared in Phase A : Architecture Vision

▪ Mapping to ... : — Mapping to Architecture ... — Mapping to reference .. — Mapping to .. — ... assessment : What all can be referred ? Start this list in Phase A. Keep updating in Phases B to D.

▪ ....analysis : Work to do and work done till now. Periodically updated in each Phases of B to D and even within its sub-work versions such as 0.2 to 1.0 .

▪ ....assessment : See **4.2.18 Requirements Impact Assessment**[5]

▪ ... Architecture : Gets its importance from Phase E. but initial observations get added even in Phases prior to that.

Read the details in this portion to obtain a better idea of the contents of this 'deliverable' document. Note that it is created in Phase A – Architecture vision as an outline but is taken through Phase C and D for getting links filled against ABBs generated therein. This document is further referred to in Phase E to F and transition states get inserted only in Phase E and f

Answer : B

––––––––––

Q 703 Which of the following is typically the final step in development of Architecture in Phase B or Phase C ?

A. Conduct formal stakeholder review

B. Create Architecture Definition Document

C. Perform gap analysis

D. Select reference models, viewpoints, and tools

---

5. **https://pubs.opengroup.org/togaf-standard/architecture-content/chap04.html#tag_04_02_18**

Explanation :

The final step is numbered 9, though steps need not be executed in exact sequence.

Answer Choice B) : This is step 9. This answer is true for Phase C (Data and Application portions) and Phase D and Phase B also

Steps in each of B D A T segment are :

▪ Select .... tools : Look into areas of the Viewpoints while narrowing down to the Stakeholders to focus upon. Make a list of (third party) Reference Models and Reference Materials to be used during the sliced work on this Architecture. Are you ready and familiar with the (soft as well as software) Tools to be deployed during such a work ?

▪ Develop .. Description : Semi-complete or partial Architecture portions (as of previous version slice in current work or reusable from earlier Projects) may be useful towards further work on these current Portfolios.

▪ Develop ... Description : The Building Blocks (ABBs) to be taken up is to be narrowed down from a suggested list of TOGAF® or stated from anything that is from the Need List of the EA Team.

▪ Perform ... : Building Blocks (in the form of Catalog / Matrix / Diagram) along with supplementing documentation is prepared. In this process the ADD – Architecture Definition Document and ARS – Architecture Requirement Specification gets enriched to the extent of work done in this version slice.

▪ Define ... components : Assess the relative priority of the Project Portfolio and Project version slices and take stock.

▪ Resolve ... Landscape : Proposed Architecture and the way it connects with other Architectural segments (among B D A T) is to be discussed towards Impact Resolution. Two way impact and immediate realignment is needed.

▪ Conduct ... review : Conduct a Review with the relevant Stakeholders, towards fit for purpose and meeting the motivational Requirements, for the portion that is proposed as Architecture right now.

▪ Finalize the ...Architecture : Seniors in EA Team accept the finalization at this stage, making sure the Impacts, Reviews and so on are duly completed.

▪ Create the **Architecture Definition Document** : Update the ADD – Architecture Definition Document and ARS – Architecture Requirement Specification to the extent of work done and duly reviewed and approved within EA department.

For example, this step is detailed in **7.3.9 Create / Update the Architecture Definition Document**[6] : under 7.3 Steps[7] :

Document the .... for ... decisions in the Architecture Definition Document. Prepare the ..... sections of the Architecture Definition Document, comprising some or all of :

▪ .... Model : What is the Business model for which this Capability enhancement is attempted ?

▪ ... model : What are the logical elements of data involved here ?

---

6. https://pubs.opengroup.org/togaf-standard/adm/chap07.html#tag_07_03_09

7. https://pubs.opengroup.org/togaf-standard/adm/chap07.html#tag_07_03

▪ Data... process model : Does it involve OLTP (On Line Transaction Processing, OLAP (On Line Analytical Processing) and so on ?

▪ ... matrix : Match the data potion to the business functional need.

▪ ... interoperability requirements (e.g., ... policies) : How do the Components here interoperate with other related Components ?

▪ If appropriate, use .... incorporate feedback : Note about the supplemental items mentioned here. What is asked to be demonstrated ?

Here we see as how we will have document the reason – rationale – for the decisions made regarding (Architectural) Building Blocks.

If you are keen on knowing as to what could be seen in such a documentation, it will be about :

▪ Business data model that is being followed in preparing the ABBs

▪ Logical data model that is prepared in Phase C, Application (and parallelly in Data) Architecture work

▪ Data management process model that will emerge as mentioned in the line above

▪ Data Entity / Business Function matrix which can be drawn an Artifact, and which can be reusable in further architecture work and so is really a Building Block

▪ Data interoperability requirements (e.g., XML schema, security policies) : Which are taken in Phase C as an ABBs and in Phase E as interoperable SBBs

Answer : B

Q 704 Which among the following statements about patterns is NOT correct ?

A. Pattern is "an idea that has been useful in one practical context and will probably be useful in others"

B. Patterns are considered to be a way of putting Building Blocks into context

C. Patterns can tell when, why, and what trade-offs you have to make

D. These are a package of functionality defined to meet business needs across an organization

E. Patterns offer the promise of helping the architect to solutions that have been proven to deliver effective in the past

Explanation :

Answer Choice D is about Building Blocks, not Patterns. All other Answer Choices do pertain to the nature of patterns.

See : **4.1.1 Background**[8] : 4. Architecture Patterns : ADM Techniques portion of TOGAF® Standard Fundamental Content Version 10

---

8. https://pubs.opengroup.org/togaf-standard/adm-techniques/chap04.html#tag_04_01

A "pattern" has been defined as : ".... useful in others" (Source : ..).

In the TOGAF® standard, patterns are considered to be a .... into context; for example, ... to a problem. Building .... are what you use : patterns can tell you ... them, ..., ..., and ...you have to make in ... Patterns offer the promise of .... to identify ....of ... and/or ... (../..) that have .... to deliver ... in the past, and may provide the ... in the future. : Make note of every point. Do they apply only to ABBs and useful during the ABB creation ?

We get to know here that a pattern is a conceptual idea. It has been found to be useful in one or more earlier contexts as a path towards a particular solution to the problem in that context.

Do read more about patterns as detailed in this section.

Important points to get to know include :

TOGAF® emphasizes that patterns reveal one approach to plan and make the Building Blocks in the context of what (Application / Data / Infrastructure) modelling is aimed at.

When it comes to considering alternative in architecture, patterns do come in handy. They may guide us in arriving at decisions on : when, why, and what trade-offs to make.

Patterns further give us the confidence to look into and narrow down to the combinations of Architecture and/or Solution Building Blocks (ABBs/SBBs). This is so because patterns are well proven concepts and ideas. They have recorded to have delivered proper and fit solutions in the past. These are sufficient reasons to consider the pattern for our immediate need now.

Looking at portions from : **4.1.3.1 Architecture Patterns and Design Patterns**[9] : 4. Architecture Patterns[10] : ADM Techniques portion of TOGAF® Standard Fundamental Content Version 10

▪ An **Architecture Pattern** expresses .... or ... for software systems. It provides a set of ..., specifies their ..., and includes ... and ... for organizing the ... between them : Structural. Over large portions of the architecture as a big picture. Like Tier, Layer, Broker Patterns.

An **Architecture Pattern** : It is about the very basic and fundamental way a software system can be structured. It would thus focus on connections between subsystems (say Layer, Tier, Client-Server through Broker and so on). Beyond providing the structure, these category of patterns would step into the defining the responsibility of each such architectural element (say Front Tier, Data Access Layer, RPC in Broker and so on) and will extend to give out the relationships between them and the rules thereon. Many of the specialized Patterns such as Microservice Patterns and Cloud Native Patterns, Cloud Architecture Patterns, Data Pipeline Pattens and so on are built upon the fundamental idea of Architectural Patterns.

We can confidently take the Architectural Pattern to be not just high level among patterns but as one which spreads itself all over the architectural activity. They are applicable irrespective of programming language or even design specific approaches. Use them to structure the entire architecture of a project and do get into Design Pattern at the next level of detailing.

---

9. **https://pubs.opengroup.org/togaf-standard/adm-techniques/chap04.html#tag_04_01_03_01**

10. https://pubs.opengroup.org/togaf-standard/adm-techniques/chap04.html#tag_04_01

▪ A **Design Pattern** provides a … for refining the … or … of a software system, or the .. between them. It describes a …. of communicating components that … within a particular context : Like GOF – Gang Of Four Patterns.

A **Design Pattern**, on the other hand will limit itself to provide the structural scheme that details the way the subsystem or the components which reside in them. Let us note that patterns such as the GOF Design Patterns do confine themselves to regularly encountered common problem areas in the design process and they provide a solution that has meaning only in the context of that design related problem (like Factory to create objects efficiently, Mediator as a one point controller or Proxy as a placeholder to lie as an intermediate component and so on). Most of them are aimed at a structure of communicating components with behavioural and relationship aspects.

And so, design pattern can be leveraged to arrive at a systematic approach to providing the name and take it forward to stimulating the motivation to use a specific design solution. It rides on the advantage of a time proven line of approach to that specific problem situation. It nudges us towards re-use of a familiar piece of design.

Take the design patterns to be a broad basis of bases of answer to questions that might crop up during the ABB creation. It can be of help during Peer Review (Resolve Impact across Architectural Landscape) and in winning the confidence of the Stakeholder during Review of the architecture at various stages in Phases B to D.

▪ An **Idiom** is a .. specific to a …. An idiom describes how to … or the …. between them using the features of the ….. : Like virtual keyword and its relevance in different programming languages with highly language specific feature.

An **Idiom**, which is less referred in the subject of patterns still is categorized as a low-level pattern. They are applicable to a specific programming language (say virtual inheritance from multiple base classes in C++, quoted string literals as Interned Memory objects in Java and Dot Net and so on).

Idioms are meant for last mile Designers and first mile programmers, helping them in resolving many issues that implementation specific. These could be on areas such as memory management in C++, or Garbage Collectors in Java and Dot Net, DOM or Web Assembly in Web Browser applications,

Note the clear distinction between the implementation level use of idioms as compared to design patterns, which have their focus on omnibus and universal structural principles. Idioms can get into more basic usage issues such as conventions in naming programme components, formatting and presenting source text, and so on. In short, idioms get us into a higher level of skill usage when it comes to issues regarding optimum use of features of programming language or development platform.

Answer : D

––––––––––––––––––

Q 705 While resolving impacts in Application Architecture by consulting B, D, T Segment Architects, the one which is not mentioned as 'should be examined' is

A. Impact on any pre-existing architectures

B. Impact on external elements that lie outside the enterprise

C. Opportunities to leverage work from this Application Architecture in other areas of the organization

D. Recent changes been made that might impact the Application Architecture

Explanation :

See : **7.3.6 Resolve Impacts Across the Architecture Landscape**[11]

The work of a segment architecture (B D A T segments) is not produced and approved in isolation. They need a Peer Review among the segments architects in the team. So, whenever Application Architecture is being finalized, the same is to be studied and resolved (with impacts on the segment work, if any) across the landscape – meaning in consultation with B, D T segment architects and the work being produced by them.

Read the five points appearing in the link above to understand the mechanism of Impact Resolution and the questions that will arise during this process.

Even if the impact relating to external elements that lie outside the enterprise could be a possibility to be examined, this question pertains to what is **mentioned as 'should be examined'** as per TOGAF® documentation ONLY.

Answer : B

Q 706 While conducting Formal Stakeholder Review in Application Architecture portion, the point herein that is not mentioned by TOGAF® is

A. Checking the original motivation for the architecture project and the Statement of Architecture Work against the proposed Application Architecture

B. Conducting an impact analysis, to identify any areas where the Business and Data Architectures may need to change to cater for changes in the Application Architecture

C. Identifying any constraints on the Technology Architecture that is about to be designed

D. Voting of the proposals by Stakeholders

Explanation :

See **7.3.7 Conduct Formal Stakeholder Review**[12]

The Enterprise Architect has to go back to the relevant Stakeholder after preparing the necessary target architectural work. That proposed output needs to be cross-checked with the original concern of the stakeholder. Further it has to be aligned to be in conformance with the Request for Architecture (motivation for the architecture project as seen in Preliminary Phase) and the Statement of Architecture Work (prepared in Phase A : Architecture Vision, specifically for a portfolio and project)

Even the Impact Analysis referred to in explanation of previous question appears in this section. Read it clearly.

There is a further mention of identifying the constraints on the Technology – Infrastructure Architecture that is being designed

There is no mention of any majority based voting in this process.

---

11. https://pubs.opengroup.org/togaf-standard/adm/chap07.html#tag_07_03_06

12. https://pubs.opengroup.org/togaf-standard/adm/chap07.html#tag_07_03_07

Answer : D

Q 707 The step of Finalizing the Application Architecture involves only one of the following combination as best way to proceed

A. Finalizing all work products using gap analysis technique; Re-using from reference models; Documenting each Building Block; Final cross-check process; Final Traceability report; Final mapping within the Architecture Repository

B. Finalizing all work products including SBBs using gap analysis technique; Re-using from reference models; Documenting each Building Block; Final cross-check process; Final Traceability report; Final mapping within the Architecture Repository

C. Finalizing all work products using gap analysis technique; Re-using from reference models but not the patterns; Documenting each Building Block; Final cross-check process; Final Traceability report; Final mapping within the Architecture Repository

D. Finalizing all work products using gap analysis technique; Re-using from reference models; Documenting each Building Block; Final cross-check process; Final Traceability report; Final mapping within the Enterprise Continuum

Explanation :

See **7.3.8 Finalize the Application Architecture**[13]

Studying this will make it clear to us that Answer Choices B) C) and D) are not in accordance.

The points in this step boils down to following sub-steps :

- Selecting the applicable standards for each of the Building Block; That too without overlooking the possibility reusing (from our own existing Landscape as also) from the reference models that are available and thus selected from the Architecture Repository
- Completing the documenting of the same, point it from the ADD – Architecture Definition Document and incorporating additional portions in the ARS – Architecture Requirements Specification
- Going for a last minute cross-check; Involves validating the proposal of architecture against business requirements; adding the reason and justification thereon in the documentation
- Incorporating the finalized requirements (means additions to the ABBs as created now) in the existing requirements traceability report
- Mapping of the emerging ABBs of the architecture suitability within the Architecture Repository on the Architecture Landscape section of it; this being a opportunity for future re-use, identify such possible needs as they are being published in the Architecture Repository
- These sub-steps signaling the finalize all the (ABB level) work products. Note that the main work product in Phases B to D are filling up the necessary pieces of architecture, known as the gap

Answer : A

---

13. https://pubs.opengroup.org/togaf-standard/adm/chap07.html#tag_07_03_08

Q 708 Phase C involves some combination of Data and Application Architecture, in either order. Advocates exist for both sequences. Data Driven approach is recommended for the situation where

A. Database and Data Warehousing is involved

B. In all projects

C. In certain key applications forming the core underpinning of the mission-critical business processes, and take the implementation and integration of those core applications as the primary focus of their architecture effort (the integration issues often constituting a major challenge)

D. CRM (Customer Relationship Management) kind of ERP (Enterprise Resource Planning) applications which come as packed COTS (Commercially Off The shelf) software

Explanation :

Answer Choices A and B are **not correct.** Every IT application may fit into these

Answer Choice C is about Application driven systems

See **5.2 Approach**[14] appearing in 5. Phase C : Information Systems Architectures under Architecture Development Method part of TOGAF® Standard Fundamental Content Version 10

Get to know the situations in which Data Architecture may get precedence and the situations where Application Architecture will get the precedence, when Phase C is approached

Answer : C

Q 709 Not an objective of Application Architecture Phase

A. Develop Target Application Architecture in a way that addresses the Statement of Architecture Work and stakeholder concerns

B. Develop Target Application Architecture in a way that addresses the Request for Architecture Work as a single Target

C. Develop Target Application Architecture in a way that enables the Business Architecture and the Architecture Vision

D. Identify candidate Architecture Roadmap components based upon gaps between the Baseline and Target Application Architectures

Explanation :

Answer Choice B) : this assumes that all the long term (say five year) goals as per Request for Architecture Work is taken up as one long project portfolio. This is totally **wrong**

See **7.1 Objectives**[15] of 7. Phase C : Information Systems Architectures — Application Architecture under Architecture Development Method part of TOGAF® Standard Fundamental Content Version 10

---

14. https://pubs.opengroup.org/togaf-standard/adm/chap05.html#tag_05_02

The objectives of the Application Architecture part of Phase C : are basically

- To develop the Target Application Architecture as needed. It should be such that it furthers and enables the Business Architecture. The Business Architecture is however based on the Architecture Vision. The Vision that is prepared along with the Statement of Architecture Work would reflect the stakeholder concerns
- To identify, meaning to arrive at the Architecture Roadmap components proposed as ABB candidates at this stage. These components in turn have to be based upon gaps between the Baseline and Target Application Architectures that is connected with this phase and the relevant iteration into this Phase

Also note that objectives of Phase B and Phase D are somewhat similar in wording. Visit the following :

4.1 Objectives[16]

6.1 Objectives[17]

7.1 Objectives[18]

8.1 Objectives[19]

Answer : B

Q 710 Application Architecture resources in the Architecture Repository as mentioned does not include

A. Generic business models and related application models relevant to the organization's industry sector

B. Application models relevant to common high-level business functions, such as electronic commerce, supply chain management, etc.,

C. Reference Model for Integrated Information Infrastructure (III-RM) — that focuses on the application-level components and services necessary to provide an integrated information infrastructure

D. The TM Forum — www.tmforum.org —detailed applications models relevant to the Telecommunications industry

Explanation :

Answer Choice D) : These were specific examples mentioned in TOGAF® 9.2 documentation. These specifics are removed in TOGAF® 10 documentation

What we see under Application Architecture portion is :

7.5.1 Architecture Repository[20]

---

15. https://pubs.opengroup.org/togaf-standard/adm/chap07.html#tag_07_01

16. https://pubs.opengroup.org/togaf-standard/adm/chap04.html#tag_04_01

17. https://pubs.opengroup.org/togaf-standard/adm/chap06.html#tag_06_01

18. https://pubs.opengroup.org/togaf-standard/adm/chap07.html#tag_07_01

19. https://pubs.opengroup.org/togaf-standard/adm/chap08.html#tag_08_01

20. https://pubs.opengroup.org/togaf-standard/adm/chap07.html#tag_07_05

This portion of ADM documentation in Phase C : Application Architecture mentions about the possible resources that are supposed to be available in the Architecture Repository.

We find a mention about the Generic business models. We need to base our application architecture work by looking into such business models and also by referring into all related application models. These are often specific and relevant to the industry sector of the Enterprise.

More mention is about the Application models relevant to the top level business functions. Examples given here are electronic commerce, supply chain management, etc.,

It is important to note that III-RM, The Open Group has a Reference Model for Integrated Information Infrastructure (III-RM) — is very much applicable to application architecture work. This is because our work and this reference model both focus on the application-level components and application level services. These two are very much necessary to provide an integrated information infrastructure.

Answer : D

Q 711 Not a Recommended artifact of Application Architecture in Phase C

A. Software Distribution Diagram

B. Enterprise Manageability Diagram

C. Product Lifecycle Diagram

D. Application Communication Diagram

Explanation :

Product Lifecycle Diagram is part of Business Architecture output. Read all under

3.6.3 Phase B : Business Architecture[21] : 3. Architectural Artifacts under Architecture Content part of TOGAF® Standard Fundamental Content Version 10

All others are recommended artifacts for Application Architecture portion of Phase C.

See : **7.4 Outputs**[22]. It merely mentions that :

The TOGAF® Standard — Architecture Content contains a detailed description of architectural artifacts which might be produced in this phase.

Now see : **3.6.5 Phase C : Application Architecture**[23] : 3. Architectural Artifacts under Architecture Content part of TOGAF® Standard Fundamental Content Version 10

▪ Catalogs :

---

21. https://pubs.opengroup.org/togaf-standard/architecture-content/chap03.html#tag_03_06_03

22. https://pubs.opengroup.org/togaf-standard/adm/chap07.html#tag_07_04

23. https://pubs.opengroup.org/togaf-standard/architecture-content/chap03.html#tag_03_06_05

Two catalogues mentioned. Think about their usage

▪ Matrices :

Four matrices mentioned. Think about their usage

▪ Diagrams :

Eight Diagrams mentioned. Do you find placement of some of them in your work in this Phase ?

Also getting to know about Product Lifecycle Diagram (from **3.6.3**[24] referenced above) **:** This diagram shows the possible state transitions of a business product, from its creation or receipt to its sale, disposal, or destruction.

Note : Those who deal with PLM – Product Lifecycle Management work on this in detail

Answer : C

———————

Q 712 Not a Recommended artifact of Application Architecture in Phase C

A. Application / Organization Matrix

B. Role / Application Matrix

C. Application / Function Matrix

D. Capability / Organization Matrix

E. Application Interaction Matrix

Explanation :

Capability / Organization Matrix is part of Business Architecture output. Read all under

3.6.3 Phase B : Business Architecture[25] : 3. Architectural Artifacts under Architecture Content part of TOGAF® Standard Fundamental Content Version 10

All others are recommended artifacts for Application Architecture portion of Phase C**.**

See : **7.4 Outputs**[26] : It merely mentions that :

The TOGAF® Standard — Architecture Content contains a detailed description of architectural artifacts which might be produced in this phase.

Now see : **3.6.5 Phase C : Application Architecture**[27] : 3. Architectural Artifacts under Architecture Content part of TOGAF® Standard Fundamental Content Version 10

---

24. https://pubs.opengroup.org/togaf-standard/architecture-content/chap03.html#tag_03_06_03

25. https://pubs.opengroup.org/togaf-standard/architecture-content/chap03.html#tag_03_06_03

26. https://pubs.opengroup.org/togaf-standard/adm/chap07.html#tag_07_04

27. https://pubs.opengroup.org/togaf-standard/architecture-content/chap03.html#tag_03_06_05

▪ Matrices :

Four matrices mentioned. What could be the idea behind TOGAF® suggesting each of them ?

Also getting to know about Capability / Organization Matrix (**from 3.6.3**[28] **referenced above**) : The purpose of this matrix is to show the organization elements that implement each capability.

The Capability / Organization matrix includes the following metamodel entities :

- ... Capability
- .... Stream
- ... Unit

Answer : D

Module 8 : Phase C : Data Architecture portion of Information Systems Architecture

———

Note that questions do come up with answer choices and correct answer picked up from other modules beyond these. Revisit all questions after revising the whole of TOGAF®.

Cross References shown as 'See' herein refer to the **6. Phase C: Information Systems Architectures — Data Architecture**[1] under Architecture Development Method part of TOGAF® Standard Fundamental Content Version 10

In case any other free-standing document of TOGAF® Standard Fundamental Content Version 10 or Series Guide is referenced, that is explicitly mentioned.

Q 801 Complete the sentence : In Phase C, when an existing application is to be replaced, the Data Architecture should _____

A. be re-factored to align with the technology infrastructure

B. describe how this change impacts other projects

C. identify the data migration requirements

D. include the application interoperability requirements

E. estimate the effort required to overcome any issues

Explanation :

When an existing application is replaced, there will naturally be a need to move and migrate data (master, transactional, and reference) to the new application. The Data Architecture is the one that should identify data migration requirements. This includes providing architectural output (ABBs) which deal with the level of transformation (in data formats and content), weeding -cleansing (scrubbing and eliminating non-correct and unwanted data). The resulting ABBs must present data in a format that is in line with the requirements and constraints of the target application.

See this in **6.5.2.2 Data Migration**[2] appearing under **6.5 Approach**[3]

The Data Architecture should .... requirements and also provide .... as to the ... transformation,.... and .... that will be required to .... in a format that meets the ...and ... of the target application. The objective being that the .... has ... when it ... Another key consideration is to ensure that an .... is established to support the transformation : Note about the operations needed and about the transformation needs.

On incorrect answer choices :

---

1. https://pubs.opengroup.org/togaf-standard/adm/chap06.html

2. https://pubs.opengroup.org/togaf-standard/adm/chap06.html#tag_06_05_02_02

3. https://pubs.opengroup.org/architecture/togaf9-doc/arch/chap09.html#tag_09_05

Aligning Data Architecture to technology architecture is a need for any project, not necessarily for existing application replacement situation only.

Application interoperability is about things like EAI – Enterprise Application Integration, SOA etc., it is not an issue of Data Architecture only.

Effort estimation is a different task and is not related to Phase C.

Answer : C

Q 802 According to TOGAF®, in which sequence should Application Architecture and Data Architecture be developed in Phase C ?

A. Application Architecture should be developed first, then Data Architecture

B. Application Architecture should be developed concurrently with Data Architecture

C. Data Architecture should be developed first, then Application Architecture

D. Application Architecture and Data Architecture may be developed in either sequence

Explanation :

Even sequence within Phase C matters. Though it can be in either sequence between Application and Data portions, a few guidelines direct us appropriately.

Do understand that both Data and application-based approach to Solution Architecture is clubbed into one Phase C only because the design of each is highly inter-related to the other.

See **5.2 Approach**[4] under **5. Phase C : Information Systems Architectures**[5] under Architecture Development Method part of TOGAF® Standard Fundamental Content Version 10

Phase C involves .... order. Advocates exist for ....

For example, ... a data-driven approach.

On the other hand, ...

Refer back to explanation appearing under **Q 701**

Note the combined Objective of Phase C as : **5.1 Objectives**[6] : 5. Phase C : Information Systems Architectures under Architecture Development Method part of TOGAF® Standard Fundamental Content Version 10

▪ Develop the Target ..., describing ..., in a way that ..

▪ Identify candidate .. based upon gaps between the .... Architectures

---

4. https://pubs.opengroup.org/togaf-standard/adm/chap05.html#tag_05_02

5. https://pubs.opengroup.org/togaf-standard/adm/chap05.html

6. https://pubs.opengroup.org/togaf-standard/adm/chap05.html#tag_05_01

Answer : D

———————

Q 803 Which are the Key Considerations for the Data Architecture ?

A. Data Analysis, Data Integrity and Data Security

B. Data Management, Data Integrity and Data Governance

C. Data Management, Data Migration and Data Governance

D. Data Analysis, Data Migration and Data Governance

E. Data Analysis, Data Integrity and Data Governance

Explanation :

Data Management, Data Migration and Data Governance are ones clearly mentioned in TOGAF® as Key Considerations.

It is better to study the tasks of Architect under these considerations.

See and study : **6.5 Approach**[7]

6.5.1.1 Data Management : When an enterprise has .... transformation, it is important to .... and ... data management issues. A ...and ...... approach to data : Study the nature of Data Management. This enables the effective use of data to capitalize on its competitive advantages.

6.5.1.2 Data Migration : When an .... is replaced, there will be a .. to migrate ... to the ... application. The Data Architecture should .... requirements and also provide .... as to the .... transformation,.... and .... that will be required to .... in a format that meets the r...and ... of the target application. The objective being that the .... has ... when it .... Another ... is to ensure that an .... is established to support the transformation : Note about the operations needed and about the transformation needs.

6.5.1.3 Data Governance : Data governance considerations ensure that the .... in place to ... : : Make a note that this is also a key consideration. It ensures that the right 'dimensions' and directions are followed while data is architectured.

Answer : C

———————

Q 804 Data Architecture resources in the Architecture Repository are mentioned to be in particular as

A. Current project Building Blocks as work in progress

B. Generic data models relevant to the organization's industry "vertical" sector

C. Energistics —Data Exchange Standards for the Upstream Oil & Gas Industry and The ARTS Operational Data Model and the ARTS Data Warehouse Model (Retail)

---

7. https://pubs.opengroup.org/togaf-standard/adm/chap06.html#tag_06_05

D. National Information Exchange Model (US Government)

Explanation :

For Answer Choice A : Such materials are stored as work in progress in Architecture Requirements Repository and not in Architecture Repository.

See : **13. ADM Architecture Requirements Management**[8] under Architecture Development Method part of TOGAF® Standard Fundamental Content Version 10

This mentions about such a Requirements Repository

Answer Choices C) and D) : These were specific examples mentioned in TOGAF® 9.2 documentation. These specifics are removed in TOGAF® 10 documentation

What we see under Data Architecture portion is :

6.5.3 Architecture Repository[9]

As part of this phase, the architecture team will need to consider ..... are available in the ...; in particular, ...relevant to the ...

Also see : **6.2 Enterprise Continuum and Architecture Re-Use**[10]

Examples of .... and ... are the wide variety of .... and ... that exist, and are continually emerging, including those that are .... (such as the ...); those specific to certain ... (such as a ..., or a ... architecture); those specific to certain types of ..., such as ..., ..., etc.; and those specific to certain ..., such as the models generated by .... like the ... (in the ... sector), ...(...), ... (..), etc., : Note what it says about internal architecture and solution artifacts. Note what all available and think about their re-use potential. Note what it says about their evolution. The first three left-hand side sections of the Enterprise Continuum are really not prepared by the Enterprise but comes from the (IT) industry at large.

Answer : B

––––––––––––

Q 805 Baseline Architecture to look for in Data Architecture does not include

A. What is already available in Architecture Landscape from previous projects

B. What is already available in Architecture Landscape from previous iteration of same project or portfolio

C. All ABBs completed in Data Architecture work

D. What is partly completed as Data Architecture work piece and is referred to by the Requirements Repository

Explanation :

What is completed and approved is one that has reached the Target needs of current project.

8. https://pubs.opengroup.org/togaf-standard/adm/chap13.html

9. https://pubs.opengroup.org/togaf-standard/adm/chap06.html#tag_06_05_03

10. https://pubs.opengroup.org/togaf-standard/architecture-content/chap06.html#tag_06_02

At best it can be used as Baseline for future projects as a re-use purpose. In current project, it is no longer be the Baseline.

The iterations in B – C – D are meant to take the Architecture work in that Domain (Data Architecture domain in this case) towards completion of ABB work. Thereafter only Phase E works on these targets and they do not need a Baseline that demands more work in any of Phase B, C, D. The Data Architecture mentioned in Answer Choice C) is part of this completion and there will be no more Baseline that needs to move towards a target.

Also See : **6.3.2 Develop Baseline Data Architecture Description**[11]

Develop a ... the existing .., to the extent ....

The scope and level of detail to be defined will depend on ....

To the extent possible, identify the ..., drawing on the ...

Baseline means :

A specification of what is available now after due review and approval.

Since the same has been prepared (in same project -portfolio or in an earlier one which is implemented) and has been agreed upon, it is taken as the basis for any more of architectural development.

Develop here means identifying such architecture as available in approved state and preparing its specifications (if not already existing).

Note that in some cases, it can be Target first and Baseline next[12], where we may have to suit the Baseline requirement so suit what is already decided as the target. This may happen with packaged software or with adaptation of an Industry specific architecture.

Answer : C

———

Q 806 Not a Recommended artifact of Data Architecture in Phase C

A. Data Dissemination Diagram

B. Data Entity / Business Function Matrix

C. Functional Decomposition Diagram

D. Data Security Diagram

Explanation :

Functional Decomposition Diagram is part of Business Architecture output. Read all under

See : **Functional Decomposition Diagram**[13] under **3.6.3 Phase B : Business Architecture**[14] : 3. Architectural Artifacts under Architecture Content part of TOGAF® Standard Fundamental Content Version 10

---

11. https://pubs.opengroup.org/togaf-standard/adm/chap06.html#tag_06_03_02

12. https://pubs.opengroup.org/togaf-standard/applying-the-adm/chap02.html#tag_02_04

The purpose of the .... diagram is to show on .... the capabilities of an organization that are .... By examining the ... from a ....., it is possible to quickly develop ... of what the .... without being ... on how the organization does it.

Once a basic Functional Decomposition diagram has been developed, it becomes possible .... to show .... and ... For example, the ... program.

All others are recommended (suggested but not mandated) artifacts for Data Architecture portion of Phase C : **Try to get to know each of the artifacts, not just here for Data Architecture but also for similar ones in other Phases. Note that all are suggested and not mandated.**

See : **6.4 Outputs**[15]. It merely mentions that :

The TOGAF® Standard — Architecture Content contains a detailed description of architectural artifacts which might be produced in this phase.

Now see : **3.6.4 Phase C : Data Architecture**[16] : 3. Architectural Artifacts under Architecture Content part of TOGAF® Standard Fundamental Content Version 10

▪ Catalogs : Study about what is appearing here. - Data Entity/Data Component Catalog

What information can architecture work get from this Catalog ?

▪ Matrices :

.. Function matrix

.. Data matrix

Think how and when these could be useful

▪ Diagrams :

Six diagrams mentioned. Do you see for some or all of them in your work area ?

Answer : C

———————————

Q 807 Not a Gap relating to Data

A. Not needed for any REST process

B. Not located where needed

C. Not available when needed

D. Not yet logically designed

---

13. https://pubs.opengroup.org/togaf-standard/architecture-content/chap03.html#tag_03_06_03_19

14. https://pubs.opengroup.org/togaf-standard/architecture-content/chap03.html#tag_03_06_03

15. https://pubs.opengroup.org/togaf-standard/adm/chap06.html#tag_06_04

16. https://pubs.opengroup.org/togaf-standard/architecture-content/chap03.html#tag_03_06_04

Explanation :

Typically, REST is only meant for data transfer and it is possible for a set of data not to be part of any REST process. (RepresEntational State Transfer)

5. Gap Analysis[17] : ADM Techniques portion of TOGAF® Standard Fundamental Content Version 10 says

The technique known as gap analysis is .... in the TOGAF® ... Method (ADM) to ... that is being developed. The basic premise is to .... Architecture; that is, items that have been .... : What is its purpose ? What is its basic premise ?

We see under **5.1 Introduction[18]: 5. Gap Analysis** : ADM Techniques portion of TOGAF® Standard Fundamental Content Version 10 says

A key step in validating an architecture is to ..... The architecture must support all of the .... needs of the organization. The most critical source of gaps that should be considered is .... work : What is the key step ? What is it supposed to support and which are the critical ones to be considered ?

Types of data gap : **Get to know each type of Gap, including what is appearing here as Data Gap**

Data ... needed Not ... needed Data ... needed

Data ... Data ... Data ...

etc.

Answer : A

Q 808 Impact of Data Architecture work need not be checked with outputs of ..

A. Preliminary Phase

B. Phase B

C. Non-data portion of Phase C

D. Phase D

Explanation :

Impact Analysis is carried out systematically in B, C and D Phases. In Phase D, Impact is checked with respect to rest of B A T domains. Preliminary Phase is not a B D A T related phase.

See : **6.3.6 Resolve Impacts Across the Architecture Landscape[19]** : What is involved in resolving impact ? Impacts across what ? Also study similar steps in B, A, T segments

Once the Data Architecture is finalized, it is necessary to .... or implications.

17. https://pubs.opengroup.org/togaf-standard/adm-techniques/chap05.html

18. https://pubs.opengroup.org/togaf-standard/adm-techniques/chap05.html#tag_05_01

19. https://pubs.opengroup.org/togaf-standard/adm/chap06.html#tag_06_03_06

At this stage, other ... in the Architecture .... should be examined to identify :

- Does this ... create an impact on ... ? : Architecture proposed now, does it clash with or complement all existing architectures with which it has a connection ?

- Have recent ...that impact on the ... ? : Does any work that is implemented recently has any impact on the current proposal ? They could have crossed each other unnoticed, since that has happened over same span of time interval.

- Are there any opportunities to ... from this .... Architecture in other areas of the organization ? : What are the re-use possibilities of the current proposal ? Building Blocks, as per TOGAF®, must be potentially re-usable.

- Does this .... impact other projects (including .... in progress) ? : Architectures are not developed in isolation. Does the current work in this segment has any impact on any work (in-progress or recently finished and pending finalization) on any other segment (among B, D, A, T segments) ? Since EA department is in charge of all architectural developments going on parallel, this kind of impact check is possible.

- Will this ...Architecture be impacted by other projects (including ... as well as those ...) ? : Architectures are not developed in isolation. Does any work (in-progress or recently finished and pending finalization) in this segment or any other segment (among B, D, A, T segments) has any impact on the current proposal ? Since EA department is in charge of all architectural developments going on parallel, this kind of impact check is possible. A corollary of point that appeared just above.

Similarly, Business Architecture in Phase B, Application Architecture in Phase C and Technology Architecture in Phase D will resolve impacts of architectural work therein with Data Architecture.

Answer : A

———————————

Q 809 Stakeholder Review at Data Architecture stage does not involve

A. Revisiting and refining the Data Architecture work

B. Looking into Data utilization along with the Stakeholders

C. Looking into original motive against current Data Architecture

D. Looking into Data Reference materials along with the Stakeholders

Explanation :

Reference materials are relevant only to Enterprise Architect and Segment and Solution Architects. Usually the Stakeholders may not use it during a review of Architecture work being presented to them for a sign-off.

Also read **6.3.7 Conduct Formal Stakeholder Review**[20]

Check the .... project and the ... Work against the ...Architecture. Conduct an ... to identify any areas where the .... Architectures (e.g., ... practices) may need to .... to cater for ... Architecture (for example, ...) : To check what against what ? To conduct what ? (Hint : **4.2.18 Requirements Impact Assessment**[21] : What are the examples given here ? Also read similar steps in B, A, T segments appearing under respective chapters under corresponding Phases of B to D.

If the .... significant, this may warrant the .... being revisited : What to revisit, when ?

Identify any areas where the .... (if generated at this point) may need to .....to cater for changes in the ...Architecture (or to identify .... about to be designed) : What is the identification and action mentioned here ?

If the impact is significant, it may be appropriate to .... of the .. at this point : See how it talks about iteration between Data and Application Architectures till all impacts are resolved.

Identify any constraints on the Technology Architecture about to be designed, refining the proposed Data Architecture only if necessary : What constrains are to be recognized here and what could be action thereon ? See how infrastructure architecture is also connected to Data Architecture here.

This review is done to satisfy what is in : **6.3.1.1 Determine Overall Modeling Process**[22]

For each viewpoint, select the .... to support the ..., using the ... tool or method : Note the emphasis on Modelling Tools and appropriate methodologies. Could be Data Modelling tools to arrive at Data storage structures and relationships, Data transmissions, Data Warehousing and Analytics and so on. (Similar ones on Application Architecture could be UML Tools / C4 tools, DDD - Domain Architecture and so on and all of them do have alignment lines with what we do here in data design)

Ensure that all .... are covered. If they are not, create ..... to address ....not covered, or ... models.

Answer : D

———————

Q 810 Not part of the Sub Step : Finalize DA portion of Architecture Definition Document

A. Documenting yet to be covered Gaps

B. Looking into Impact Reports

C. Looking into Application Interoperability

D. Looking into Data Store, Data Transport, Data Transformation issues

Explanation :

The Sub Steps are understood, on seeing **6.3.8 Finalize the Data Architecture**[23] Also make it a point to study and analyze similar steps in B, A, T segments appearing under respective chapters under corresponding Phases of B to D.

▪ Select ...., re-using as much as possible from the ... selected from the .. Repository : Making proper use of standards and reference models available.

▪ Fully .... Block : Documentation needs.

21. https://pubs.opengroup.org/togaf-standard/architecture-content/chap04.html#tag_04_02_18

22. https://pubs.opengroup.org/togaf-standard/adm/chap06.html#tag_06_03_01_01

23. https://pubs.opengroup.org/togaf-standard/adm/chap06.html#tag_06_03_08

▪ Conduct a .... of overall architecture against ...; document the ... document : More checks the better. That also lead to better documentation of the rationale and reasons behind each selection made in the architecture work.

▪ Document the .... report : Traceability is necessary in future to play back the navigation the steps across ADM taken now.

▪ Document the .... of the architecture within the ...Repository; from the ..., identify those that ..., and publish via the ... Repository : Publish suitably. Moving form Requirement Repository to Architecture Landscape section of the Architecture Repository may happen here.

▪ Finalize all the ..., such as .. : Anything more ? Complete them.

6.3.9 Create the Architecture Definition Document[24] deals with Data Interoperability and not Application Interoperability **:** Also make it a point to study and analyze similar steps in B, A, T segments appearing under respective chapters under corresponding Phases of B to D.

Document the .... decisions in the ... Document : Note the documentation discipline expected. Where is it documented ? (Do study all about Architecture Definition Document and Architecture Requirements Specification. Very important in TOGAF® and as the main output pieces of ADM)

Application interoperability is dealt as per : **7.4 Outputs**[25] : 7. Phase C: Information Systems Architectures — Application Architecture under Architecture Development Method part of TOGAF® Standard Fundamental Content Version 10

: The outputs of Phase C (Application Architecture) may include,

Draft Architecture ... as **:** — ... interoperability ...

Data interoperability is dealt as per **6.4 Outputs**[26]

Answer : C

Q 811 When using the ADM to establish an Architecture Capability, which phase would define the structure of the organization's Architecture Repository ?

A. Application Architecture

B. Business Architecture

C. Data Architecture

D. Preliminary Phase

E. Technology Architecture

Explanation :

---

24. https://pubs.opengroup.org/togaf-standard/adm/chap06.html#tag_06_03_09

25. https://pubs.opengroup.org/togaf-standard/adm/chap07.html#tag_07_04

26. https://pubs.opengroup.org/togaf-standard/adm/chap06.html#tag_06_04

The Data Architecture would define the structure of the organization's Architecture Repository and hence the indexed accessing logic of Enterprise Continuum. This means the task of setting up an Architecture Repository and a (portal style Content management System to access it as) Enterprise Continuum lie with Data Architect.

Get to know about all four domain roles in : **2.1 Overview**[27] : 2. Establishing an Architecture Capability : Enterprise Architecture Capability and Governance part of TOGAF® Standard Fundamental Content Version 10

As with any business capability, the establishment of an .... Capability can be supported by the ...Method (...) : There are many 'Capabilities' in an Enterprise. Architecture Capability is one of them, but is important to us since TOGAF® is meant to enhance that capability only.

Successful use of the ... will provide a ..., ..., and ... that enables the ..., helps ... the value of ... and pro-actively identifies ... to gain ... and manage ... : See the multivarious facets of one aspect known a Capability.

Implementing any capability ... require the design of :

▪ The **Business Architecture** ...

▪ The **Data Architecture** ...

▪ The **Application Architecture** ...

▪ The **Technology Architecture** ..

Answer : C

———————————

Q 812 Which of the following is not part of the TOGAF® Data Architecture ?

A. Data entity / business function matrix

B. Conceptual data models

C. Data dissemination view

D. Data lifecycle view

E. Query optimization plans

Explanation :

Query optimization plans is not among Data Architecture functionalities indicated in TOGAF®. It can be included in the tailored TOGAF® for the Enterprises which feel the need for it. Or it may already be there hidden among the other outputs of this phase.

Data Architecture outputs include, as per: **3.6.4 Phase C : Data Architecture**[28] : 3. Architectural Artifacts under Architecture Content part of TOGAF® Standard Fundamental Content Version 10

---

27. https://pubs.opengroup.org/togaf-standard/ea-capability-and-governance/chap02.html#tag_02_01

28. https://pubs.opengroup.org/togaf-standard/architecture-content/chap03.html#tag_03_06_04

▪ Catalogs :

— .... catalog

▪ Matrices :

— ... matrix — .. matrix

▪ Diagrams :

— .. diagram — ... diagram — ..diagram

— ... diagram — ... diagram — .. diagram

See explanation appearing under **Q 806**

Answer : E

———————

Q 813 Which one of the following is NOT an objective for Phase C, Data Architecture ?

A. Defining an architecture that can be understood by the stakeholders

B. Defining an architecture that is complete and consistent

C. Defining an architecture that is stable

D. Defining data entities that are normalized to minimize update anomalies

E. Defining data entities relevant to the enterprise

Explanation :

Defining data entities that are normalized to minimize update anomalies is not seen in the list of Objectives for Data Architecture given by TOGAF°.

See : **6.1 Objectives**[29]

Develop the .. that enables the .... Architecture and the Architecture ...., in a way that .... the ... ... and ... : Focus on how work done in Vision and Business Architecture are taken forward, not missing out on concerns of the stakeholders and the need to address the tasks promised in the Statement of Architecture Work that is prepared and approved in Phase A. Will the stakeholder be different here and the concerns be different ? Yes. We will go through this chapter to get to know about it.

Identify candidate .... components based upon ... the ...and ... Architectures : Focus on what components of the Roadmap, this time pertaining to data area that are to be identified and worked on. That is based on another set of Gaps.

It also pays to read : **6.5 Approach : 6.5.1 Key Considerations for Data Architecture**[30]

———————

29. https://pubs.opengroup.org/togaf-standard/adm/chap06.html#tag_06_01

30. https://pubs.opengroup.org/togaf-standard/adm/chap06.html#tag_06_05_02

6.5.2.1 Data Management[31]

When an enterprise ...., it is important to ....

6.5.2.2 Data Migration[32]

When an existing application ..., there will be ....

6.5.2.3 Data Governance[33]

... considerations ensure that ....

See explanation appearing under **Q 803**

Answer : D

────────

Q 814 A Data Architecture should be able to handle all except

    A. Data at rest — data in stores
    B. Data in motion — data in transactions or services / APIs
    C. Data in use — data at the border of the application (e.g., GUI)
    D. Data which is deleted
    E. Open data — data that the organization provides for public usage and which it is voluntarily or legally required to provide

Explanation :

All except D is appearing in : **6.5.1 Data Structure[34]**

A Data Architecture .. to handle:

Data .. — data in ..

Data .. — data in ... (note how the parameters and information is - Micro services and API – Application Program Interfaces therein are treated)

Data ... — data at the border ...

Open data — ... for public usage ...

Answer : C

31. https://pubs.opengroup.org/togaf-standard/adm/chap06.html#tag_06_05_02_01

32. https://pubs.opengroup.org/togaf-standard/adm/chap06.html#tag_06_05_02_02

33. https://pubs.opengroup.org/togaf-standard/adm/chap06.html#tag_06_05_02_03

34. https://pubs.opengroup.org/togaf-standard/adm/chap06.html#tag_06_05_01

Q 815 Data Architecture is created by using three metamodel entities, which are all except

A. Data entity

B. Logical data component

C. Physical data component.

D. Data definition

Explanation :

See : **6.5.1 Data Structure**[35]

Data Architecture is ....

Note that actually Data definition is a part of Data Entity formulation. It is not a separate metamodel entity

Answer : D

––––––––––––––––––

Q 816 On Data Entitles : Locate the incorrect statement

A. Data entities can be used to create conceptual data models

B. These Data Entity based models are to help the IT developers understand the concepts they will be dealing with

C. Each Data Entity is a standalone and unrelated piece of concept

D. Often the entity relationship models also contain some requirements on the relations (e.g., a customer can only have one address)

Explanation :

See the full paragraph appearing in : **6.5.1 Data Structure**[36]

Data entities can be used to ...they will be dealing with.

Often the ....

Answer : C

35. https://pubs.opengroup.org/togaf-standard/adm/chap06.html#tag_06_05_01

36. https://pubs.opengroup.org/togaf-standard/adm/chap06.html#tag_06_05_01

Q 817 Spot the incorrect statement

A. Logical data components can be used to create logical data models. Often it is important for the IT area to have a clear view of all data that is used in the IT environment

B The logical data model is often used as a requirement on the data stored in applications (at rest), data moved between applications (in motion), or data at the user interface of applications (data in use)

C. Logical Data Model does not have any correlation with a Physical Data Model

D. Physical data components are clusters of logical data components that have been implemented by some earlier project (links to, for example, XML message, database schemas) or requirements for new implementation projects

Explanation :

See the full paragraph appearing in : **6.5.1 Data Structure**[37]

Logical data components .....

Often it is ....

The logical data model is ... on the data ..., data ..., or data ...

Physical data components are ...

Answer : C

---

37. https://pubs.opengroup.org/togaf-standard/adm/chap06.html#tag_06_05_01

Module 9 : Phase D : Technology Architecture

Note that questions do come up with answer choices and correct answer picked up from other modules beyond these. Revisit all questions after revising the whole of TOGAF®.

Cross References shown as 'See' herein refer to the **8. Phase D : Technology Architecture**[1] under Architecture Development Method part of TOGAF® Standard Fundamental Content Version 10

In case any other free-standing document of TOGAF® Standard Fundamental Content Version 10 or Series Guide is referenced, that is explicitly mentioned.

Q 901 In Phase D, which of the following resources from the Architecture Repository should be considered in the development of the Technology Architecture ?

A. Architecture Vision

B. Business rules, job descriptions

C. Implementation and Migration Plan

D. Stakeholder Map

E. TOGAF® Technical Reference Model

Explanation :

The TOGAF® TRM should be considered in the development of the Technology Architecture in Phase D. It also influences Phase C, especially the Application Architecture.

Look at the term : "resources from Architecture Repository" : And see what TOGAF® documentation says, as given below, at this context of "resources". If you think of any other content of Architecture Repository as a resource, do note that the way TOGAF® defines in the context here is different. Certification goes by TOGAF® documentation.

As part of Phase D, the architecture team will need to consider what relevant Technology Architecture resources are available in the Architecture Repository.

See : **8.3.2 Develop Baseline Technology Architecture Description**[2]

Begin by ... technology components (e.g., the TOGAF® Technical Reference Model (TRM)).

See : **8.5.2 Architecture Repository**[3] : Also make it a point to study similar section in B, A, D segments appearing under respective chapters under corresponding Phases of B to D.

Existing ... catalog : About various services.

---

1. https://pubs.opengroup.org/togaf-standard/adm/chap08.html

2. https://pubs.opengroup.org/togaf-standard/adm/chap08.html#tag_08_03_02

3. https://pubs.opengroup.org/togaf-standard/adm/chap08.html#tag_08_05_02

Generic technology models relevant to the organization's industry "vertical" sector : Generic one makes ideal starting point reference and helps us form ABBs.

Technology models relevant to Common Systems Architectures : Grouped components are referred to in TOGAF® as 'Common Systems'.

TOGAF® Technical Reference Model (TRM) (Note that TOGAF® aligns III-RM more with Application Architecture)

Also note : Choice A and D above is pertinent to Phase A.

Choice B is pertinent to Phase B.

Choice C is about Phase F.

Answer : E

Q 902 Enabler for moving to an execution model of Application and Data Components

A. TRM

B. III-RM

C. Phase C – Information Systems Architecture

D. Phase D – Technology Architecture

Explanation :

What is "execution model" of software application and data portion ? It is the Technology Architecture and the infrastructure like server, operation system etc., are the ones which are part of the 'execution model'.

If the question is about architecture model or design model of Application and Data, then only the other three answers relating to Phases C will step in.

Remember TOGAF® jargons :

Execution Model of Phase B : Phase C

Execution Model of Phase C : Phase D

Enterprise Project, meaning getting into Preliminary Phase

Architecture Project : Phase A onwards. Towards Phase E, they turn into Transition Architectures and get finalized in Phase F as ready for Migration project execution.

Execution (coding / testing / installation) of Migration / Realization / Implementation Project happens, usually by other agencies (such as PMO, Operations or their partner vendors from external sources) through such delivery vehicles, in parallel to Phase G.

Also see : **8.1 Objectives**[4] : The objectives of Phase D are to :

▪ Develop the ... that enables ... through ..., in a way that addresses ....

▪ Identify ...

Answer : D

———————

Q 903 Technology Architecture resources in the Architecture Repository are mentioned to be in particular as

A. Current project Building Blocks as work in progress

B. Generic data models relevant to the organization's industry "vertical" sector

C. The TM Forum — www.tmforum.org — detailed technology models relevant to the Telecommunications industry

D. No such resources exist

Explanation :

For Answer Choice A) : Such materials are stored as **work in progress in Architecture Requirements Repository** and not in Architecture Repository.

See : **13. ADM Architecture Requirements Management**[5] under Architecture Development Method part of TOGAF® Standard Fundamental Content Version 10

This mentions such a Requirements Repository

Answer Choice C) : This was a specific examples mentioned in TOGAF® 9.2 documentation. These specifics are removed in TOGAF® 10 documentation

Answer Choice D) : **Absurd** since TOGAF® mentioned quite a few resources for Technology Architecture

What we see under Technology Architecture portion is :

8.5.2 Architecture Repository[6]

As part of Phase D, the architecture team will need to consider ... are available in the Architecture Repository

In particular :

- Existing ... The .. technical reference model, ... Generic ..
- Technology models relevant to ..
    - ... (III-RM) ... — that focuses on ...

Answer : B

———————————————————————————

4. https://pubs.opengroup.org/togaf-standard/adm/chap08.html#tag_08_01

5. https://pubs.opengroup.org/togaf-standard/adm/chap13.html

6. https://pubs.opengroup.org/togaf-standard/adm/chap08.html#tag_08_05_02

Additional note :

Existing IT Services can be found and selected based on **: 7.2 Architecture Landscape**[7] : The Architecture Landscape holds .... of the ... of the enterprise at particular points in time.

TRM and Models on infrastructure as developed by the TeleManagement Forum (TMF) can be found and selected from **: 7.3 Reference Library**[8] :

The Reference Library provides a .... that should be used to ..... Reference materials held may be obtained from a variety of sources, including :

▪ ...bodies : From various standardization institutions : IEEE, ISO, ASTM, ANSI, OMG, W3C, IEC, ITU, ECMA, OASIS, WS-Integration (WS-I) and so on.

▪ .... Vendors : Every large vendor, including Cloud vendors and networking-hardware vendors and many others do have their own product and service standards. These are purely vendor-specific standards.

▪ Industry .... : Not just TMF, ARTS, Energetics, Active Store, National Information Exchange Model (US Government) etc., which are seen n TOGAF® documentation but there ae many more from : PCI DSS, HIPAA, BIAN, Petrotechnical Open Software Corporation (POSC) and a host more like these from every large vertical industry and their representative bodies. Search in internet and you will come across an endless list.

▪ ... templates : Many template area available. Some are on TOGAF® and open Group. Many more on related topics. Can serve as a first step draft to any document to be made by the Architect. For example : Volere Requirements Specification Template.

▪ Enterprise ... : If not from third party advisors, these can come from Centre of Excellence, those who make POC – Proof Of Concept architecture and so on.

The Reference Library should contain : Any relevant material that the Architect may refer when clarity is needed

▪ Reference .. : Like the IT4IT Reference Architecture from Open Group and many more like this. OMG – Object Management Group provides many for different verticals.

▪ Reference ... : A reference model is a standard decomposition of a known problem into parts that cooperatively solve the problem. Patterns, and other documentary reference materials including white papers, stock material, and guides are part of this.

▪ Viewpoint ... : Focussed libraries that pinpoint to Viewpoints of various categories of Stakeholders

▪ .... : Any other lookup and templated material.

---

7. https://pubs.opengroup.org/togaf-standard/architecture-content/chap07.html#tag_07_02

8. https://pubs.opengroup.org/togaf-standard/architecture-content/chap07.html#tag_07_03

Q 904 One that fits perfectly into Baseline Architecture of Phase D

A. Future plans of enhancement into Architecture

B. Current plans for Architecture in this iteration

C. Existing technology and architecture descriptions

D. None of the above

Explanation :

Phase D confines itself to Technology Architecture – means Infrastructure and other first tier hosting software as also the network topology or such other Cloud / internet connections. Hence existing technology and its relevant architecture descriptions will make sense there. The Architect can use existing technology for newer architecture pieces also to maintain consistency and to take advantage of spare capacity.

See : **8.3.2 Develop Baseline Technology Architecture Description**[9]

Develop a Baseline Description of the .... Architecture, to support the .. Architecture. The ... descriptions exist.

Begin by .... of the existing environment into the .... of ... and ... (e.g., the ...). This will allow the team developing the architecture to gain ... taxonomy.

The team may be able to take advantage of a ...., but it is assumed that some ... to match the ... described as part of this process. Another important task is to ... of the new architecture.

Also see : **7.2 Architecture Landscape**[10] under Architecture Content part of TOGAF® Standard Fundamental Content Version 10

The Architecture Landscape ...

Answer : C

————————

Q 905 Not a Technology Gap

A. Database yet to be designed

B. Hardware across tiers to be of uniform technology

C. Existing hardware may have spare capacity

D. None of the above are gaps

Explanation :

Database design is task of Data Architecture, Phase C

---

9. https://pubs.opengroup.org/togaf-standard/adm/chap08.html#tag_08_03_02

10. https://pubs.opengroup.org/togaf-standard/architecture-content/chap07.html#tag_07_02

Finding and filling up the gaps in Technology Architecture does include looking for hardware in various tiers, IP addresses within the Enterprise and also looking into capacity utilization of all existing hardware units.

8.3.4 Perform Gap Analysis[11] (in **Technology Architecture**)

Verify the architecture models for .... and .. :

▪ Perform ... among the different views : Select the best among the alternatives. Resolve between conflicting claims of viewpoint based concerns.

▪ Validate ..., and constraints : Recheck to see if they fall in line with Principles and Goals set in the Preliminary Phase. Look out for constraints, if any, in meeting them.

▪ Note ... from the Architecture : Viewpoint libraries and other references may be compared with.

▪ Test ... against requirements : Carryout dry run and walk through kind of testing.

Identify gaps between the ..., using the ... technique.

Do note that the Gap Analysis technique is not just to find out shortfalls (items that have been deliberately omitted, accidentally left out, or not yet defined) but also to take action such as developing the Architectural Building Blocks or procuring the corresponding Building Block.

Also note that newer Technologies also fall into the area of Gap.

8.5.1 Emerging Technologies[12]

The evolution of new technologies is a .... for change in enterprises looking for ... of ...and .. their business. The Technology Architecture needs to capture the .... available to the ....through the ...of ... : It is all towards innovation in operating and in improving business, and so transformation opportunities of state-ot-art technologies is to be leveraged. Note that 'technology' under Phase D is not just about infrastructure. It is all about hosting platforms, networks, Cloud Enablement, connectivity and more like these. In modern systems even K8S – Kubernetes kind of hosting platforms and all these which support microservices and analytics can also be taken into the span of this Phase.

While the Enterprise Architecture is led by the ...., drivers for change are often ... capabilities. As more digital innovations ...., stakeholders need to both ... and be open to ... change. Part of Digital Transformation has arisen due to the convergence of ..... and ..... which have opened up ... of ... infrastructures : Technology capability is major driver for change, say as witnessed with Cloud Enablement and many others like this. Digital innovations, and convergence of telecom enhancements (say 5G and the like) with computing capability enhancements (say IoT) only speed up this change.

Solution development methods are also ... to .... traditional ... and putting pressure on the .... and .. benefits of the ... Enterprise Architecture approach. Yet without a ... approach, the rapid ... will cause ...across the enterprise : Newer trends in DevOps and other development / deployment area also need attention.

Answer Choice D) is **factually incorrect**. All the three above are gaps.

Answer : A

---

11. https://pubs.opengroup.org/togaf-standard/adm/chap08.html#tag_08_03_04

12. https://pubs.opengroup.org/togaf-standard/adm/chap08.html#tag_08_05_01

Q 906 Not to be treated as an impact respect to Technology Architecture output

A. High Security coming in way of performance

B. Installation may require a shut-down of operations

C. Business LOB users deciding on the Technology to be used

D. Governance has directed to expand to newer Technology areas

Explanation :

While doing impact analysis of newly introduced target Technology Architecture, Business (LOB - Line Of Business) users have very little say on the kind of technology as it is beyond their sphere of knowledge. General guidelines on technology selection may appear in Architecture Principles and Technology Principles therein.

However, Answer Choices of A, B and D do fall into the sphere of impact analysis in Technology Architecture.

3.6.5 Phase C : Application Architecture[13] **: Software Engineering Diagram :** talks of a diagram that is useful with impact analysis starting from Phase C (Do read about all artifacts of all Phases appearing here sometime or other)

The Software Engineering diagram .....

It enables ... analysing opportunities and solutions.

These are at : **3. Architectural Artifacts**[14] under Architecture Content part of TOGAF® Standard Fundamental Content Version 10

8.3.6 Resolve Impacts Across the Architecture Landscape[15] (in **Technology Architecture**) details it as :

Once the Technology Architecture is finalized, ...

At this stage, .. to identify :

▪ Does this Technology Architecture ... ?

▪ Have .. impact the Technology Architecture ?

▪ Are there any ... in other areas of the organization ?

▪ Does this Technology Architecture .. ?

▪ Will this Technology Architecture be ... ?

Do study a similar step discussed in a different but comparable context appearing under **Q 808**

Answer : C

---

13. https://pubs.opengroup.org/togaf-standard/architecture-content/chap03.html#tag_03_06_05

14. https://pubs.opengroup.org/togaf-standard/architecture-content/chap03.html

15. https://pubs.opengroup.org/togaf-standard/adm/chap08.html#tag_08_03_06

Q 907 Not a Diagram produced in Phase D

A. Platform Decomposition Diagram

B. Software Engineering Diagram

C. Network and Communications Diagram

D. Processing Diagram

Explanation :

See : **3.6.6 Phase D : Technology Architecture**[16] : 3. Architectural Artifacts under Architecture Content part of TOGAF® Standard Fundamental Content Version 10

List of Diagrams, recommended to be produced in Phase D are :

— .. and Locations diagram : What all would it depict ?

— Platform .. diagram : What details would it convey ?

— Processing ... : About what kind of process ?

— Networked ... diagram : Which part of networking does it involve ? Does it cover over the internet and into he cloud ?

— Network and .... diagram : Which other part of networking does it involve ?

The recommendation under Phase C, Applications Architecture does include Software Engineering Diagram. It is **not under** Technology Architecture.

Better to get to know each Phase and the artifacts recommended therein.

3.6.6 Phase D : Technology Architecture[17] referred to above details as :

Platform Decomposition Diagram[18] : depicts the technology platform ...

The diagram covers ...and provides ....

The diagram can be expanded to ... within a specific ...

Network and Communications Diagram[19] : describes ... in the Technology Architecture; insofar as ...

Processing Diagram[20] : focuses on ...

A deployment unit ....

---

16. https://pubs.opengroup.org/togaf-standard/architecture-content/chap03.html#tag_03_06_06

17. https://pubs.opengroup.org/togaf-standard/architecture-content/chap03.html#tag_03_06_06

18. https://pubs.opengroup.org/togaf-standard/architecture-content/chap03.html#tag_03_06_06_05

19. https://pubs.opengroup.org/togaf-standard/architecture-content/chap03.html#tag_03_06_06_08

20. https://pubs.opengroup.org/togaf-standard/architecture-content/chap03.html#tag_03_06_06_06

Answer : B

Q 908 Which Architecture domain describes logical software and hardware capabilities ?

A. Application Architecture

B. Business Architecture

C. Data Architecture

D. Information Systems Architecture

E. Technology Architecture

Explanation :

The Technology Architecture, as per TOGAF®, is something more than mere Infrastructure Architecture. It actually includes the software (meaning operating system and all middleware that supports the Application and Data components as the first tier of hosting) and hardware (including network, datacentre / cloud and all such) capabilities that are ultimately needed to support the deployment of all envisaged services.

It does mention 'business services' since the architecture part of setting up Call Centres, Chat Bots, RPA (Robotic Process Automation) and things such as these which are needed to support the business activity do come under EA role.

Hence Technology Architecture scope includes IT infrastructure, middleware, networks, communications, processing, and standards. All standards (of hardware and supporting software) components are drawn up under Technology Architecture.

8.1 Objectives[21] :

▪ Develop the ... that enables ... to be delivered through .., in a way that ..

▪ Identify ...

8.3.1.1 Determine Overall Modeling Process[22] : includes points such as

The process to develop ... steps :

▪ Define ... ▪ Identify ... ▪ Carry out ...

▪ Look at ... ▪ Is the ... ?

— Refine the ..

— ... selection (including ...)

▪ Determine .. ▪ Determine ..:

---

21. https://pubs.opengroup.org/togaf-standard/adm/chap08.html#tag_08_01

22. https://pubs.opengroup.org/togaf-standard/adm/chap08.html#tag_08_03_01_01

— ... and ...

— ...planning

— ... impacts

Do study a similar step discussed in a different but comparable context appearing under **Q 703**

Answer : E

———————————

Q 909 Which one of the following describes a key objective of the Technology Architecture Phase ?

A. To define the solution architecture needed to support the Application Architecture

B. To define technology components into a set of technology platforms

C. To define the Transition Architectures needed to achieve the Target Architecture

D. To develop a migration plan to deliver incremental capabilities

E. To select a set of technology products that will form the basis of a solution architecture

Explanation :

To define the solution architecture needed to support the Application Architecture - Phase C : Note the word 'define'.

To define the Transition Architectures needed to achieve the Target Architecture - Phase E.

To develop a migration plan to deliver incremental capabilities – Phases E and F.

To select a set of technology products that will form the basis of a solution architecture – Phases E and F; Phase D stops with architectural design which is ABBs and does not go into SBBs.

8.1 Objectives[23] :

▪ Develop ....

▪ Identify ...based upon ...

Objectives of phases, important from Certification point of view.

Answer : B

---

23. https://pubs.opengroup.org/togaf-standard/adm/chap08.html#tag_08_01

Some questions hereon may be in the combined areas of Phase B, Phase C and Phase D or even other phases.

Q 910 Which of the ADM phases includes the development of Application and Data Architectures ?

A. Phase A

B. Phase B

C. Phase C

D. Phase D

E. Phase E

Explanation :

In TOGAF®, Phase C is said to include the development of both Application and Data Architectures. Some Enterprises have even separated them as Phase C1 and C2 when they tailored the TOGAF®.

See : **5.2 Approach**[24] : Phase C : Information Systems Architectures under Architecture Development Method part of TOGAF® Standard Fundamental Content Version 10

Phase C involves .. of Data and Application Architecture, in ...

Some guidelines in going for Data / Application first is also given therein as : For example, ..recommends a data-driven approach.

On the other hand, ... — often provide a combination of ..., and some organizations take .., whereby they recognize .., and take the .. as the primary focus of ..

Also see : **5.1 Objectives**[25] : Phase C : Information Systems Architectures under Architecture Development Method part of TOGAF® Standard Fundamental Content Version 10

▪ Develop the ..., describing how the .. will enable .., in a way that ..

▪ Identify ...

Answer : C

Also note from : **5.2.2 Essential ADM Output and Knowledge : Table 4**[26] of TOGAF® Series Guide : A Practitioners' Approach to Developing Enterprise Architecture Following the TOGAF® ADM

Phase B, Phase C, and Phase D : Output & Outcome

A set of .. approved by the .. for the .., with a set of ..., and work to ...

————————————————

24. https://pubs.opengroup.org/togaf-standard/adm/chap05.html#tag_05_02

25. https://pubs.opengroup.org/togaf-standard/adm/chap05.html#tag_05_01

26. https://pubs.opengroup.org/togaf-standard/adm-practitioners/adm-practitioners_5.html#_Ref490978563

Q 911 Which architecture domain is the first architecture activity undertaken in the ADM cycle ?

A. Application

B. Business

C. Data

D. Technology

Explanation :

Business Architecture is undertaken first so as to demonstrate the business value of subsequent architecture work to key stakeholders. In other words, all the architecture work done in Phases C to D are in furtherance of the requirements documents in Phase B, these being ones done with business value generation and capability enhancement in mind.

A reason for something to be the first architecture activity can be only because what it provides. It provides the basis for further works. Not because it focusses, defines, finalizes or mobilizes, since these can be provided by any other Architectures – such as Data, Application, Technology etc.,

See : **4.5.1 General**[27] : 4. Phase B: Business Architecture : under Architecture Development Method part of TOGAF® Standard Fundamental Content Version 10

A knowledge of the Business Architecture is a .... in any other ... and is therefore ..., if not catered for already ... : Important point.

In practical terms, the Business Architecture is also ...means of demonstrating ... to ..., and the ... from ..

Also look at **Figure 2-1 : Iteration Cycles**[28] and be convinced as to who the Architecture Development Iteration starts from Phase B.

This is at **2.2 Iteration Cycles**[29] : 2. Applying Iteration to the ADM under Applying the ADM part of TOGAF® Standard Fundamental Content Version 10 :

Answer : B

––––––––––––––––––––

Q 912 Complete the sentence : The process of managing architecture requirements applies to_____ ?

A. All ADM phases

B. The Preliminary Phase

C. Phase A : Architecture Vision

D. The Requirements Management phase

27. https://pubs.opengroup.org/togaf-standard/adm/chap04.html#tag_04_05_01

28. https://pubs.opengroup.org/togaf-standard/applying-the-adm/chap02.html#tagfcjh_1

29. https://pubs.opengroup.org/togaf-standard/applying-the-adm/chap02.html#tag_02_02

Explanation :

Architecture Requirements are managed across all phases of the ADM.

Vision Phase only initiates it with aspirational Vision.

Requirement Management Phase only manages the flow of Requirements between phases.

Preliminary Phase is more about overall initiative and does not look into stakeholder requirements for specific projects. Preliminary Phase is one of Enterprise Project, meaning no specific project in mind but the goals to address pain points (initiatives for an Architectural Movement) are defined.

See : **13.4 Outputs**[30] : 13. ADM Architecture Requirements Management under Architecture Development Method part of TOGAF® Standard Fundamental Content Version 10

When .... is generated, which identifies the .. to address the changes.

The statement goes through .... of the requirements (e.g., ...) on the architecture development. Once requirements for the current ADM cycle have been finalized then the .... should be updated : What are the 'implications' mentioned here ? What is updated as per this portion and when ?

Also see under : **13.5.1 General**[31] : 13. ADM Architecture Requirements Management under Architecture Development Method part of TOGAF® Standard Fundamental Content Version 10

Note also that ... process itself does not ...; this is done within the ....

It is merely .. for ..

Answer : A

———————

Q 913 According to TOGAF®, which of the following steps in Phases B, C, and D occur before development of the baseline or target architectures ?

A. Conduct formal stakeholder review

B. Create Architecture Definition Document

C. Define Roadmap components

D. Perform gap analysis

E. Select reference models, viewpoints and tools

Explanation :

Steps in each phase is important and the steps repeat in Phases B to D. Focus on them.

The steps in Phases B, C, D read as :

---

30. https://pubs.opengroup.org/togaf-standard/adm/chap13.html#tag_13_04

31. https://pubs.opengroup.org/togaf-standard/adm/chap13.html#tag_13_05_01

▪ Select „,

▪ Develop Baseline .... Architecture Description

▪ Develop Target .... Architecture Description

▪ Perform ... ▪ Define ... ▪ Resolve ..

▪ Conduct .. ▪ Finalize the .... Business Architecture

▪ Create the ...

These are the way we are stepping though (not necessarily in the same exact sequence) Phases B, C, D : Phases known as B D A T : Business Architecture (Phase B), Data and Application Architectures (Phase C), Technology Architecture (Phase D)

Also read the explanation appearing under **Q 703**

Answer : E

———————

Q 914 Which of the following is the architecture domain of TOGAF® that describes the logical software and hardware capabilities ?

A. Application Architecture

B. Business Architecture

C. Data Architecture

D. Technology Architecture

E. Infrastructure Architecture

Explanation :

TOGAF® used the term "Technology Architecture" to refer to the domain that describes the logical software and hardware capabilities. "Infrastructure Architecture" could be the term used in some Enterprises to refer to hardware capabilities. Note that in TOGAF® this includes logical software (operating system and other platform tools) also and is known as Technology Architecture.

See under : **3.3 What Kind of Architecture Does the TOGAF® Standard Deal With ?**[32] 3. Core Concepts under Introduction and Core Concepts part of TOGAF® Standard Fundamental Content Version 10

The **Technology Architecture** describes ....

In same section other Architectural Domains (rest of B A D T) gets mentioned as ;

▪ The **Business Architecture** defines ..

———

32. https://pubs.opengroup.org/togaf-standard/introduction/chap03.html#tag_03_03

- The **Data Architecture** describes ...

- The **Application Architecture** provides ...

8.1 Objectives[33] :

- Develop the .. enables ... to be delivered through ..., in a way that ...

- Identify ... components based upon ...

Answer : D

Q 915 Which one of the following is considered a relevant architecture resource in Phase D ?

A. Generic application models relevant to the organization's industry sector

B. Generic business models relevant to the organization's industry sector

C. Generic data models relevant to the organization's industry sector

D. Generic technology models relevant to the organization's industry sector

Explanation :

Generic technology models which are relevant to the industry sector of the Enterprise are appropriate resources in Phase D. We only prepare ABBs here which have a tone of generic and abstract nature in them.

It is nice to get know about nature of such resources by reading details quoted below.

See : **8.5.2 Architecture Repository**[34]

As part of Phase D, the architecture team will ... are available in the ....

In particular :

- Existing ... • The adopted ... • Generic ...

- Technology models relevant to ..

— ... (III-RM) — see the TOGAF® Series Guide: **The TOGAF® Integrated Information Infrastructure Reference Model**[35]

— ... (III-RM) — that focuses on ..

Note : TRM, Technical Reference Model is a more relevant resource for Phase D and a separate Series Guide is available. Somehow the above section has missed mentioning the same.

See about such Series guide here.[36]

---

33. https://pubs.opengroup.org/togaf-standard/adm/chap08.html#tag_08_01

34. https://pubs.opengroup.org/togaf-standard/adm/chap08.html#tag_08_05_02

35. https://pubs.opengroup.org/togaf-standard/reference-models/iiirm.html

Answer : D

––––––––––––

Q 916 In Phases B, C, and D, which is the final step in each phase ?

A. Conduct formal stakeholder review

B. Create Architecture Definition Document

C. Define Roadmap components

D. Perform gap analysis

E. Select reference models, viewpoints and tools

Explanation :

The steps in Phases B, C, D read as :

▪ Select ...

▪ Develop ... . Architecture Description

▪ Develop ... . Architecture Description

▪ Perform ... ▪ Define ... ▪ Resolve ...

▪ Conduct ... ▪ Finalize the .... .. Architecture

▪ Create the ...

This last step, details, depending on the Phase, something like : **4.3.8 Finalize the Business Architecture**[37] : 4. Phase B : Business Architecture : under Architecture Development Method part of TOGAF® Standard Fundamental Content Version 10

▪ Select standards ..., re-using .. from ..

▪ Fully ...each Building Block ▪ Conduct a ...against ..; document the ...

▪ Document the ... ▪ Document the ...; from the , identify ...., and publish ..

▪ Finalize ..

Answer : B

––

36. https://www.opengroup.org/togaf-series-guides

37. **https://pubs.opengroup.org/togaf-standard/adm/chap04.html#tag_04_03_08**

Q 917 In Phases B, C, and D of the ADM cycle the first step defined is to select reference models, viewpoints, and tools. Which of the following is the next step in each of these phases ?

A. Conduct formal stakeholder review

B. Create Architecture Definition Document

C. Develop Baseline Architecture

D. Perform gap analysis

E. Resolve impacts across the Architecture Landscape

Explanation :

The steps in Phases B, C, D read as :

- Select ...

- Develop ... . Architecture Description

- Develop ... . Architecture Description

- Perform ...

- Define ...

- Resolve ...

- Conduct ...

- Finalize the .... .. Architecture

- Create the ...

These steps are not necessarily to be executed in the same order. But we have listed the way they are appearing in TOGAF® documentation and in most cases the same serial path is followed.

This step, details, depending on the Phase something like : **4.3.2 Develop Baseline Business Architecture Description**[38] : 4. Phase B : Business Architecture : under Architecture Development Method part of TOGAF® Standard Fundamental Content Version 10

Develop a ... of the ..., to the ....

The scope and level of detail to be defined will depend on ...

Where new architecture models need to be developed ..., use the ....

Answer : C

_____

38. https://pubs.opengroup.org/togaf-standard/adm/chap04.html#tag_04_03_02

Q 918 In which part of the ADM cycle are Building Blocks evolved using a common platform of steps ?

A. Preliminary Phase and Phase A

B. Phases B, C and D

C. Phases E and F

D. Phases G and H

Explanation :

Phases B, C and D of ADM have almost identical steps, forming as a common platform.

Study the steps in :

4.3 Steps : Of Phase B[39]

6.3 Steps : Of Phase C, Data Architecture[40]

7.3 Steps : Of Phase C, Application Architecture[41]

8.3 Steps : Of Phase D[42]

▪ Select ...

▪ Develop ... . Architecture Description

▪ Develop ... . Architecture Description

▪ Perform ... ▪ Define ... ▪ Resolve ...

▪ Conduct ... ▪ Finalize the .... .. Architecture

▪ Create the ...

Also read the explanation appearing under **Q 703**

Answer : B

––––––––––––––––––

Q 919 Which of the following is a Key Point of the ADM Cycle ?

A. Though ADM is iterative, the decisions regarding enterprise coverage, level of detail, time period and architecture asset re-use needs to be taken upfront

B. ADM provides a recommended the scope of activity which can be tailored by the organization itself

---

39. https://pubs.opengroup.org/togaf-standard/adm/chap04.html#tag_04_03

40. https://pubs.opengroup.org/togaf-standard/adm/chap06.html#tag_06_03

41. https://pubs.opengroup.org/togaf-standard/adm/chap07.html#tag_07_03

42. https://pubs.opengroup.org/togaf-standard/adm/chap08.html#tag_08_03

C. Where necessary, use of the ADM should be tailored to meet the needs of the organization but phases cannot be omitted

D. The main guideline is to focus on what creates value to the enterprise, and to select horizontal and vertical scope, and project schedules, accordingly

E. Decisions taken should be based on the value accruing to the enterprise only

Explanation :

The main guideline and key point of ADM is to focus on what creates value to the enterprise, and to select horizontal and vertical scope, and project schedules, accordingly. While every Answer Choice could be true in applying themselves to the ADM Cycle, **the question is about the Key Point.**

1.8 Summary[43] **: 1 Introduction :** under Architecture Development Method part of TOGAF® Standard Fundamental Content Version 10

The TOGAF® ADM defines a .... for the various phases and steps involved in developing an architecture, but it .... a scope — this has to be ... by the organization itself, bearing in mind that the ... in the ADM process is an ..., with the depth and ... increasing with each iteration.

Each iteration will add ... to the organization's Architecture Repository. While a ... is useful (indeed, essential) to have in mind as the ...., in practice there is a **key decision** to be made ...of a specific ... effort. This being the case, it is vital to .. on which ... are being made, and to set ... for what is the .. effort.

The main guideline is to focus on what creates value to the enterprise, and to .... scope, and .... accordingly. Whether or not this is the.... understand that this ... repeated, and that future .... on what is being created in the .., adding ...

Whether or not this is the first time around, ...

Answer : D

———

Q 920 How is the scope of the architecture projects decided ?

A. Agreement on the scope is reached in the Preliminary phase but the definition happens through phase A to D

B. The scope is defined in the Preliminary phase and agreement is reached in the same phase

C. The scope is defined in phase A and refined in phases B, C and D

D. Agreement on the scope is reached in the Preliminary phase and is defined in phase A

E. The scope is defined and agree upon in the Preliminary phase

Explanation :

Architecture projects are those which start in Phase A and get matured in the subsequent phases of ADM. So, they have the scope defined in Phase A and then get refined in phases B, C and D.

43. https://pubs.opengroup.org/togaf-standard/adm/chap01.html#tag_01_08

See : **2.5.3 Requirements for Architecture Work**[44] : **2. Preliminary Phase** under Architecture Development Method part of TOGAF® Standard Fundamental Content Version 10

The business imperatives ....

They should be ...

See : **3.3.6 Define Scope**[45] : 3. Phase A: Architecture Vision under Architecture Development Method part of TOGAF® Standard Fundamental Content Version 10

Define what .. and what is .., understanding that the ....

See : **4.5.1 General**[46] : 4. Phase B : Business Architecture : under Architecture Development Method part of TOGAF® Standard Fundamental Content Version 10

The scope of work in Phase B is ... as set out in ....

The business strategy defines ..., but not necessarily .....

That is the role of the ....

See steps in Phases C and D which talk about the "scope".

Answer : C

---

44. https://pubs.opengroup.org/togaf-standard/adm/chap02.html#tag_02_05_03

45. https://pubs.opengroup.org/togaf-standard/adm/chap03.html#tag_03_03_06

46. https://pubs.opengroup.org/togaf-standard/adm/chap04.html#tag_04_05_01

Module 10 : Architecture Partitioning

———

Note that questions do come up with answer choices and correct answer picked up from other modules beyond these. Revisit all questions after revising the whole of TOGAF®.

Cross References shown as 'See' herein refer to

4. Architecture Partitioning[1] under Applying the ADM part of TOGAF® Standard Fundamental Content Version 10

Or

3. Applying the ADM Across the Architecture Landscape[2] under Applying the ADM part of TOGAF® Standard Fundamental Content Version 10

Or

7. Architecture Repository[3] under Architecture Content part of TOGAF® Standard Fundamental Content Version 10

The prefix such as **4.** Or **3.** Or **7.** Will help you locate the right reference.

In case any other free-standing document of TOGAF® Standard Fundamental Content Version 10 or Series Guide is referenced, that is explicitly mentioned.

Q 1001 What are the levels of granularity Architecture Landscape is divided into ?

A. Strategic Architectures, Segment Architectures and Capability Architectures

B. Strategic Architectures, Segment Architectures and Transition Architectures

C. Enterprise Architectures, Segment Architectures and Capability Architectures

D. Enterprise Architectures, Segment Architectures and Transition Architectures

E. Enterprise Architectures, Solution Architectures and Transition Architectures

Explanation :

The three, as per TOGAF® are : Strategic Architectures (long term), Segment Architectures (mid-range) and Transition Architectures (Units of Capability Increment)

3.2 Architecture Landscape[4]

---

1. https://pubs.opengroup.org/togaf-standard/applying-the-adm/chap04.html

2. https://pubs.opengroup.org/togaf-standard/applying-the-adm/chap03.html

3. https://pubs.opengroup.org/togaf-standard/architecture-content/chap07.html

4. https://pubs.opengroup.org/togaf-standard/applying-the-adm/chap03.html#tag_03_02

1. **Strategic Architecture** provides an ..... for .... and ... activity and allows for direction setting at an ... level : At (Top) executive level. Preliminary Phase will be the centre focus but it does extend a little into Phase A : Architecture Vision. Note phrases such as 'organizing framework' (all set up till Request for Architecture Work is formulated) and 'change activity' (Goals set to relive Pain Point and to take advantage of modernizing the business and technology engagement).

2. **Segment Architecture** provides an .... for ... and ... and allows for direction setting and the development of .... at a ... level : Portfolio and a set of related projects coming under a portfolio are first scoped at Phase A : Architecture Vision. Further architecture development on these is ideally happening at Phases B to D, where ABBs are developed. Roadmap Components are developed in these Phases.

3. **Capability Architecture** provides an .... for ... and the development of ... realizing .. : In TOGAF®, 'capability increment' ideally points us towards Phase E. Here SBBs are created duly aligned with Transition Architectures (each one increasing capability by some degree) and bunched under different Work Packages. These relate to Roadmap of the transition. There is a larger role for PMO and Operations department around these activities with EA department assuming and Oversight (Implementation Governance) role when the action gets final approval in Phase F and moves to Phase G.

See : **3.4 : Organizing the Architecture Landscape to Understand the State of the Enterprise**[5] :

The following characteristics are typically used to organize the Architecture Landscape :

- **Breadth:** the ..... Landscape. Architectures are functionally . or segments : Enterprise-wide scope for Long Term initiatives, then get into portfolio / project scope as per relevant step in Phase A.

- **Depth:** with .... and complexity. More ... architectures : This sets the limit on how much we should dwell in ?

- **Time:** for a ..... the future : May spill into more than one year

- **Recency:** finally, ... finally approved : Maintaining it with up-to-date enhancement requests.

Answer : A

Q 1002 What level of the Architecture Landscape provides a long-term summary view of the entire enterprise ?

A. Capability Architecture

B. Operational Architecture

C. Segment Architecture

D. Strategic Architecture

E. Tactical Architecture

Explanation :

Strategic Architecture is the one that provide view of entire enterprise. This the term uses by TOGAF® for long term initiatives.

---

5. https://pubs.opengroup.org/togaf-standard/applying-the-adm/chap03.html#tag_03_04

See under : **3.2 Architecture Landscape**[6]

1. **Strategic Architectures** show a ....summary view of the .... Strategic Architectures provide an ... for ... and ...activity and allow for direction setting at an ... level : Long Term : For entire Enterprise. Coming under Preliminary Phase and strategic portion of Phase A.

Also see : **Figure 3-1 Summary Classification Model for Architecture Landscapes**[7]

Also see : **7.2 Architecture Landscape**[8]

1) **Strategic Architectures** show ... summary view ....

Strategic Architectures provide .... for ... and allow for ..

Also see : **7.6.2 Contents of the Architecture Requirements Repository**[9]

1) **Strategic Architecture Requirements** show a ... of the requirements ....

Strategic Architecture Requirements ....

Answer : D

———————

Q 1003 Which of the architecture in different levels of granularity in architecture landscape provide view of entire enterprise ?

A. Enterprise Architecture

B. Strategic Architecture

C. Segment Architecture

D. Capability Architecture

Explanation :

Strategic Architecture provides a comprehensive view of entire enterprise and its architectural landscape in toto.

Note : Enterprise Architecture is a higher term, which is broken up into three granular levels. We will have to focus on Strategic Architecture for answer to this question, which has the phrase 'levels of granularity' in it.

See under : **3.2 Architecture Landscape**[10]

Strategic Architecture provides an .....

Also see : **Figure 3-1 Summary Classification Model for Architecture Landscapes**[11]

6. https://pubs.opengroup.org/togaf-standard/applying-the-adm/chap03.html#tag_03_02

7. https://pubs.opengroup.org/togaf-standard/applying-the-adm/chap03.html#tagfcjh_6

8. https://pubs.opengroup.org/togaf-standard/architecture-content/chap07.html#tag_07_02

9. https://pubs.opengroup.org/togaf-standard/architecture-content/chap07.html#tag_07_06_02

10. https://pubs.opengroup.org/togaf-standard/applying-the-adm/chap03.html#tag_03_02

Also see : **7.2 Architecture Landscape**[12]

1. **Strategic Architectures** show .....

Read the explanation appearing under **Q 1001 and Q 1002**

Answer : B

––––––––––––

Q 1004 Which one of the following is defined as formal description of the enterprise, providing an executive-level long-term view for direction setting ?

A. Baseline Architecture

B. Business Architecture

C. Foundation Architecture

D. Segment Architecture

E. Strategic Architecture

Explanation :

The definition of Strategic Architecture : Formal description of the enterprise, providing an executive-level long-term view for direction setting.

Read the explanation appearing under **Q 1001 and Q 1002**

The other two being :

2) **Segment Architectures** .....

Segment Architectures can be used at the ...

3) **Capability Architectures** show ... fashion how the enterprise can support a ...

Capability Architectures are used to provide an overview of ....

Answer : E

––––––––––––

Q 1005 Which level of the Architecture Landscape contains the most detail ?

A. Capability Architectures

B. Segment Architectures

C. Strategic Architectures

––

11. https://pubs.opengroup.org/togaf-standard/applying-the-adm/chap03.html#tagfcjh_6

12. https://pubs.opengroup.org/togaf-standard/architecture-content/chap07.html#tag_07_02

D. None of the above are part of the Architectural Landscape

Explanation :

Capability Architectures get into Transition Architecture and prepare SBBs, which contain the maximum of details. TOGAF® recommends that every Architecture effort started in Phase A should culminate in as many Transition Architectures as needed when they reach Phase E.

See : **7.2 Architecture Landscape**[13] :

The Architecture Landscape holds .... of the state of the enterprise at .... in time. Due to the ... and the ... throughout an entire enterprise, the Architecture Landscape is divided into ... : What does the Landscape hold ? Why is it partitioned ? Of these, the Capability Architectures which are really detailed into SBB level of Architecture with LLD – Low Level Design and gets impregnated with implementation level specifics will be the most detailed.

3. Capability Architectures show in a **more detailed fashion** how the ... a particular .... Capability Architectures are used to provide an overview of .... capability, ... capability, and .. increments and allow for .... and ... to be ...within managed ... : What are the capability states and increments mentioned here ? What do they allow for ?

Also see : **7.6.2 Contents of the Architecture Requirements Repository**[14]

　　Capability Architecture Requirements identify ....

3. Capability Architecture Requirements identify the .... for a particular .... Capability Architecture Requirements identify .... and ... to be grouped within ... and ... : Note 'detailed requirements for a particular unit of capability' – each unit being a Transition Architecture. What do they identify ?

Also see : **4.34 Capability Architecture**[15] : 4. Definitions under Introduction and Core Concepts part of TOGAF® Standard Fundamental Content Version 10

An architecture that describes .....

Read the explanation appearing under **Q 1001**

Answer : A

――――――――――

Q 1006 Complete the sentence. The Architecture Landscape is divided into three levels, Strategic, Segment and _____.

A. Baseline

B. Capability

C. Solution

---

13. https://pubs.opengroup.org/togaf-standard/architecture-content/chap07.html#tag_07_02

14. https://pubs.opengroup.org/togaf-standard/architecture-content/chap07.html#tag_07_06_02

15. https://pubs.opengroup.org/togaf-standard/introduction/chap04.html#tag_04_34

D. Target

E. Transition

Explanation :

Architecture Landscape is divided into three levels : Strategic, Segment and Capability Architecture.

See : **7.2 Architecture Landscape**[16] : The Architecture Landscape holds ... into three levels of granularity :

Strategic Architecture

Segment Architecture

Capability Architecture

Also See : **7.2 Architecture Landscape**[17] : **3. Capability Architectures** show .... a particular unit of ..

Capability Architectures are used to ...

Read the explanation appearing under **Q 1001**

Also see : **7.6.2 Contents of the Architecture Requirements Repository**[18] : **3. Capability Architecture Requirements** identify ...

Capability Architecture Requirements .....

Also see : **4.34 Capability Architecture**[19] : 4. Definitions under Introduction and Core Concepts part of TOGAF® Standard Fundamental Content Version 10

An architecture that describes ...

Answer : B

Q 1007 Which of the drivers for architectural change is top down ?

A. Incremental change

B. Strategic

C. Software methodology change

D. Enhance a technology capability

E. Changes identified during the ongoing projects

Explanation :

---

16. https://pubs.opengroup.org/togaf-standard/architecture-content/chap07.html#tag_07_02

17. https://pubs.opengroup.org/togaf-standard/architecture-content/chap07.html#tag_07_02

18. https://pubs.opengroup.org/togaf-standard/architecture-content/chap07.html#tag_07_06_02

19. https://pubs.opengroup.org/togaf-standard/introduction/chap04.html#tag_04_34

Strategic approach is for change in top down manner.

More than getting to the answer, the following deserves a study.

See **12.5.1 Drivers for Change**[20] under **12. Phase H : Architecture Change Management**[21] under Architecture Development Method part of TOGAF® Standard Fundamental Content Version 10

The main purpose for the development of the Enterprise Architecture so far has been .... and ... and ... to achieve corporate capabilities.

However, Enterprise Architecture does ..... vacuum. There is usually an ... and...which is already providing value : What could be existing already ?

There are also probably drivers for change which are often .... based upon .. to .... Enterprise Architecture .... by a strategic .... to a degree, although the .... makes the equation .... : Note about these two kind of drivers. What is said to be 'more complex' here ?

There are three ways to change the existing infrastructure that have to be integrated : **Make a note of all three ways.**

▪ ..., ... directed change to ... new capability (...) : CapEx approach.

▪ ... changes to ... or .. capability (... and ..) for infrastructure under operations management : Capacity rationalization approach.

▪ Experiences with the .... project ... in the care of ..., but still being ... projects : Reuse of Lessons Learned documents.

Answer : B

―――――――――

Q 1008 Strategic Architecture does not involve

A. Showing a long-term summary view of the entire enterprise

B. Detailed operating models for areas within an enterprise

C. Providing an organizing framework for operational and change activity

D. Allowing direction setting at an executive level

Explanation :

Strategic Architecture is not for producing detailed operating models for areas within an enterprise, which is actually a task for Segment Architecture.

See Section : **7.2 Architecture Landscape**[22]

---

20. https://pubs.opengroup.org/togaf-standard/adm/chap12.html#tag_12_05_01

21. https://pubs.opengroup.org/togaf-standard/adm/chap12.html

22. https://pubs.opengroup.org/togaf-standard/architecture-content/chap07.html#tag_07_02

The Architecture Landscape holds ... views of the ... at particular points in time. Due to the ... and the ... throughout an entire enterprise, the Architecture Landscape is ... of granularity.

Strategic Architectures show a ... of the entire enterprise. Strategic Architectures provide an ... executive level.

See under : **3.2 Architecture Landscape**[23]

Strategic Architecture provides ....

Also See : **4.77 Strategic Architecture**[24] : 4. Definitions under Introduction and Core Concepts part of TOGAF® Standard Fundamental Content Version 10

A summary ... of the enterprise, providing ... for .. and ..., and an .., .. view for ...

Also see : **Figure 3-1 Summary Classification Model for Architecture Landscapes**[25]

Answer : B

————————

Q 1009 Segment Architecture does not involve

A. Providing more detailed operating models for areas within an enterprise

B. Being used at the program or portfolio

C. Being used organize and operationally align more detailed change activity

D. Being used to provide an overview of current capability, target capability, and capability increments

Explanation :

Answer Choice D) is about Capability Architecture.

See : **7.2 Architecture Landscape**[26]

Segment Architectures provide more .... an enterprise. Segment Architectures can be used ...change activity.

Also see : **4.67 Segment Architecture**[27] : 4. Definitions under Introduction and Core Concepts part of TOGAF® Standard Fundamental Content Version 10

A ... description of ..., used at ... to ... change activity

The **change activity mentioned here is not** the changes addressed after or during an implementation. The very idea of **scope of architecture that starts from Phase A is generally mentioned as 'change activity' at various places in TOGAF®.**

23. https://pubs.opengroup.org/togaf-standard/applying-the-adm/chap03.html#tag_03_02

24. https://pubs.opengroup.org/togaf-standard/introduction/chap04.html#tag_04_77

25. https://pubs.opengroup.org/togaf-standard/applying-the-adm/chap03.html#tagfcjh_6

26. https://pubs.opengroup.org/togaf-standard/architecture-content/chap07.html#tag_07_02

27. https://pubs.opengroup.org/togaf-standard/introduction/chap04.html#tag_04_67

Also see: **3.2 Architecture Landscape**[28]

2. **Segment Architecture** provides an ... at a program or portfolio level.

Also see : **Figure 3-1 Summary Classification Model for Architecture Landscapes**[29]

Also see under : **7.6.2 Contents of the Architecture Requirements Repository**[30] :

Segment Architecture Requirements provide ....

Segment Architecture Requirements may ...

Answer : D

––––––––––––––––

Q 1010 Capability Architecture does not involve

A. Providing more detailed operating models for areas within an enterprise

B. Showing in a more detailed fashion how the enterprise can support a particular unit of capability

C. Being used to provide an overview of current capability, target capability, and capability increments

D. Allowing for individual work packages and projects to be grouped within managed portfolios and programs

Explanation :

Capability Architecture is not there to provide more detailed operating models for areas within an enterprise. In fact operating models are related to Segment Architecture.

See Section : **7.2 Architecture Landscape**[31]

Capability Architectures show ....

Capability Architectures are ...

Also see : **7.6.2 Contents of the Architecture Requirements Repository**[32] : 3. **Capability Architecture Requirements** identify ....

Capability Architecture Requirements identify ....

Also see : **4.34 Capability Architecture**[33] : 4. Definitions under Introduction and Core Concepts part of TOGAF® Standard Fundamental Content Version 10

An architecture that ...

28. https://pubs.opengroup.org/togaf-standard/applying-the-adm/chap03.html#tag_03_02

29. https://pubs.opengroup.org/togaf-standard/applying-the-adm/chap03.html#tagfcjh_6

30. https://pubs.opengroup.org/togaf-standard/architecture-content/chap07.html#tag_07_06_02

31. https://pubs.opengroup.org/togaf-standard/architecture-content/chap07.html#tag_07_02

32. https://pubs.opengroup.org/togaf-standard/architecture-content/chap07.html#tag_07_06_02

33. https://pubs.opengroup.org/togaf-standard/introduction/chap04.html#tag_04_34

Also see : **Figure 3-1 Summary Classification Model for Architecture Landscapes**[34]

Answer : A

Q 1011 Capability Architecture is useful for all except

A. Providing an overview of current capability

B. Providing an overview of long-term capability needs

C. Providing an overview of target capability

D. Providing an overview of capability increments

Explanation :

Capability Architecture is all about small transitions delivering immediate value. Hence it is not about long term capability needs.

See : **7.2 Architecture Landscape**[35]

Capability Architectures in a ....

Capability Architectures are ....

Also see : **7.6.2 Contents of the Architecture Requirements Repository**[36] : 3. **Capability Architecture Requirements** identify .....

Capability Architecture Requirements ...

Also see : **4.34 Capability Architecture**[37]: 4. Definitions under Introduction and Core Concepts part of TOGAF® Standard Fundamental Content Version 10

An architecture that ...

Also see : **Figure 3-1 Summary Classification Model for Architecture Landscapes**[38]

Also note from **4.1 Overview**[39] : 4. Architecture Patterns : ADM Techniques portion of TOGAF® Standard Fundamental Content Version 10 that

Partitions are used to simplify the development and management of the Enterprise Architecture.

---

34. https://pubs.opengroup.org/togaf-standard/applying-the-adm/chap03.html#tagfcjh_6

35. https://pubs.opengroup.org/togaf-standard/architecture-content/chap07.html#tag_07_02

36. https://pubs.opengroup.org/togaf-standard/architecture-content/chap07.html#tag_07_06_02

37. https://pubs.opengroup.org/togaf-standard/introduction/chap04.html#tag_04_34

38. https://pubs.opengroup.org/togaf-standard/applying-the-adm/chap03.html#tagfcjh_6

39. https://pubs.opengroup.org/togaf-standard/applying-the-adm/chap04.html#tag_04_01

Partitions lie at the foundation of Architecture Governance and are distinct from levels and the organizing concepts of the Architecture Continuum

Be prepared for questions on above aspects

Answer : B

————————

Q 1012 Does ADM support iteration ?

A. Yes, you can cycle around all single individual phases

B. Yes, you can only cycle around the ADM

C. Yes, you can cycle around any combination of phases

D. Yes, you can cycle around ADM, iterate across specific phases or cycle through some of the phases

E. No, ADM is not iterative

Explanation :

See : **2.1 Overview**[40] under **2. Applying Iteration to the ADM**[41] under Applying the ADM part of TOGAF® Standard Fundamental Content Version 10 : Every navigation possibility discussed below is important.

▪ Projects will exercise ... : Each cycle .... The architecture ...

▪ Separate projects ...

▪ One project may trigger ... the scope of its Request for Architecture Work

Iteration within an ADM cycle (Architecture Development iteration) :

▪ Projects may ... : Typically, ...

▪ Projects may cycle between ... : Typically, this is used ....

▪ Projects may return to .... : Typically, this is used ... of stakeholder requirements

Iteration to manage the Architecture Capability (Architecture Capability iteration) :

▪ Projects may require ... to address a Request for Architecture Work

▪ Projects may require a ... a Change Request in Phase H

Answer : D

---

40. https://pubs.opengroup.org/togaf-standard/applying-the-adm/chap02.html#tag_02_01

41. https://pubs.opengroup.org/togaf-standard/applying-the-adm/chap02.html#tag_02

Q 1013 In Phases B, C, and D, which is the first step in each phase ?

A. Conduct formal stakeholder review

B. Create Architecture Definition Document

C. Define Roadmap components

D. Perform gap analysis

E. Select reference models, viewpoints and tools

Explanation :

The steps in Phases B, C, D read as :

▪ Select ..

▪ Develop .... Description ▪ Develop ... Description

▪ Perform ... analysis ▪ Define .... components

▪ Resolve ... across the ..... ▪ Conduct .... review

▪ Finalize the .... . Architecture

This first step, details, depending on the phase as : **4.3.1 Select Reference Models, Viewpoints, and Tools**[42] 4. Phase B : Business Architecture : under Architecture Development Method part of TOGAF® Standard Fundamental Content Version 10

Select relevant .... resources (..., ... etc.) from the ...., on the basis of the ...., and the ... and ... : What all mentioned as resources ? From what architecture resources ? What are the three basis areas mentioned here ?

Select relevant Business Architecture viewpoints (e.g., ..., ..., ...); i.e., those that will .... architect to ... how the ... are being addressed in .... : Note the mention of operations, management and financials samples.

Identify appropriate .... to be used for ..., ..., and ...., in association with the ..... : The Enterprise Architects should not shy away from using Tools such as UML, C4. ArchiMate and so on. Otherwise they will look like a plumber who has forgotten to use a pipe wrench.

Depending on the ...... warranted, these may comprise .... or ...., or more .... tools and techniques, such as ....models, ... models, ... models, etc., : Note all three models.

Also go through explanation appearing under **Q 703**

This step is numbered 1, as per TOGAF®, though steps need not be executed in exact sequence

Answer : E

———————————

42. https://pubs.opengroup.org/togaf-standard/adm/chap04.html#tag_04_03_01

Q 1014 The description of future state of the architecture being developed for an enterprise is referred to as

A. Architecture Vision

B. Target Architecture

C. Strategic Architecture

D. None of the above

Explanation :

Target Architecture is always a description of what will be achieved in future at the end of some stage (future state).

Target Architecture[43] : The description of ....

Note : There may be several future states developed as a roadmap to show the evolution of the architecture to a target state.

4.3.3 Develop Target Business Architecture Description[44], taken from Business Architecture as an example, reads as :

Develop a .....

The scope and level of detail to be defined ......

To the extent possible, ...

Where new .... need to be developed to ...., use the ... to describe ...

4.22 Architecture Vision[45] helps us understand more about Target Architecture

A succinct description of the .... that describes its ... and the .....

It serves as an ....

This is at : **4. Definitions**[46] under Introduction and Core Concepts part of TOGAF® Standard Fundamental Content Version 10

Answer : B

NON-CONVENTIONAL MULTIPLE choice questions start from here. Go through them with attention since such questions are hallmark of TOGAF® 10 Exam

Some of these will involve portions from modules covered so far in the series. This should be so, because that is how a few questions may appear, testing your knowledge across Phases and across other components of TOGAF®

43. https://pubs.opengroup.org/togaf-standard/introduction/chap04.html#tag_04_78

44. https://pubs.opengroup.org/togaf-standard/adm/chap04.html#tag_04_03_03

45. https://pubs.opengroup.org/togaf-standard/introduction/chap04.html#tag_04_22

46. https://pubs.opengroup.org/togaf-standard/introduction/chap04.html

Q 1050

Consider the following statements which appear in a logical sequence from 1 to 4, look into them being true or false and then set to pick the right combination :

1 Levels and the Architecture Continuum provide a comprehensive mechanism to describe and classify the Architecture Landscape.

These concepts can be used to organize the Architecture Landscape into a set of related architectures with:

2
- Manageable complexity for each individual architecture or solution
- Defined groupings

And also with :

3
- Casual hierarchies and free-flow structures
- Appropriate processes, roles, and responsibilities which are detached from each grouping

4 There is no definitive organizing model for architecture, as each enterprise should adopt a model that reflects its own operating model.

Which deliverables match these descriptions?

A. 1 False – 2 False – 3 False – 4 False

B. 1 False – 2 False – 3 False – 4 True

C. 1 True – 2 True – 3. False - 4 True

D. 1 True – 2 True – 3 True –4 True

Explanation :

See under : **3.2 Architecture Landscape**[47]

Row 3 should read as :

And also with :

- Defined hierarchies and navigation structures
- Appropriate processes, roles, and responsibilities attached to each grouping

Answer : C

---

47. https://pubs.opengroup.org/togaf-standard/applying-the-adm/chap03.html#tag_03_02

Q 1051

This is regarding Architecture Partitioning :

Statement

1 Partitions are used to simplify the development and management of the Enterprise Architecture.

2 Partitions lie at the foundation of Architecture Governance and are distinct from levels and the organizing concepts of the Architecture Continuum.

Architectures are partitioned because :

3
- Organizational unit architectures conflict with one another
- Different teams need to work on different elements of architecture at the same time and partitions allow for specific groups of architects to own and develop specific elements of the architecture
- Effective architecture re-use requires modular architecture segments that can be taken and incorporated into broader architectures and solutions

4 It is quite possible to present a definitive partitioning model for architecture. Each enterprise needs to adopt a common partitioning model as other Enterprises that reflects its own operating model.

Check if the Statement is True or False as per following :

A. 1 – True 2 – True 3 – False 4 – True

B. 1 – False 2 – True 3 – False 4 – True

C. 1 – True 2 – False 3 – False 4 – True

D. 1 – True 2 – True 3 – True 4 – False

Explanation :

See under : **4.1 Overview**[48]

Row 4 should read as :

It is **impractical to present** a ... for architecture.

Each enterprise ... that reflects its ....

Answer : D

48. https://pubs.opengroup.org/togaf-standard/applying-the-adm/chap04.html#tag_04_01

Q 1052

Study the image :

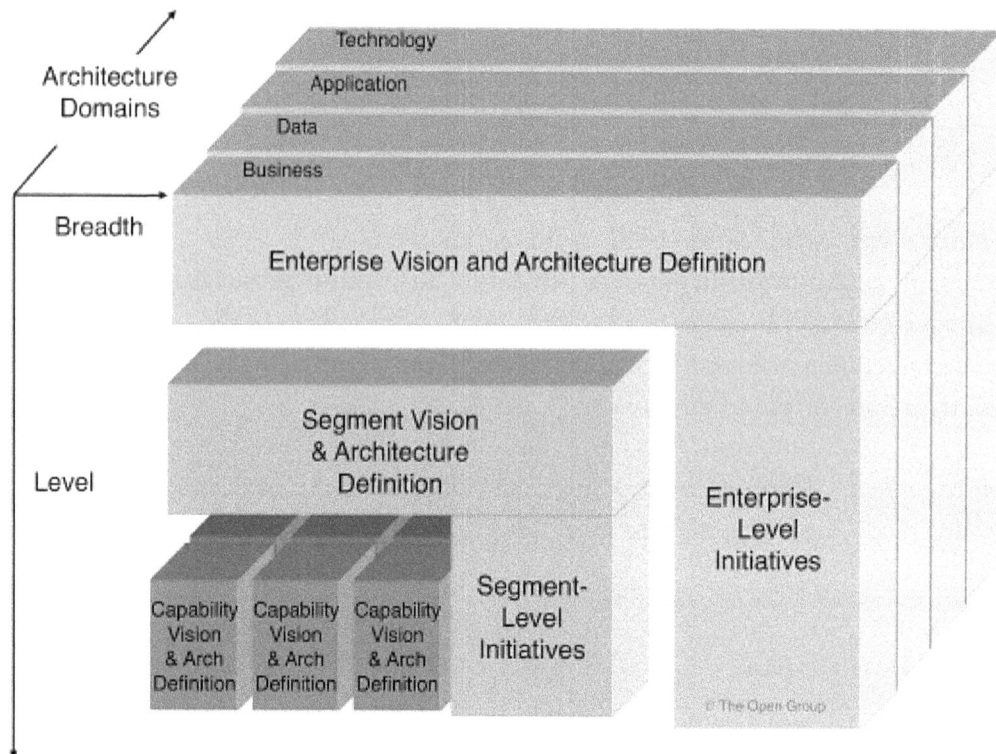

PICK THE WRONG POINT on Architecture Integration :

A. Architectures that are created to address a subset of issues within an enterprise require a consistent frame of reference so that they can be considered as a group as well as point deliverables.

B. Figure above[49] illustrates how different types of architecture will have to exist independently and in a disjoint fashion. The dimensions that are used to define the scope boundary of a single architecture (e.g., level of detail, architecture domain, etc.,) are typically the same dimensions that must be addressed when considering the integration of many architectures.

C. At the present time, the state of the art is such that architecture integration can be accomplished only at the lower end of the integratability spectrum. Key factors to consider are the granularity and level of detail in each artifact, and the maturity of standards for the interchange of architectural descriptions.

D. As organizations address common themes (such as Service-Oriented Architecture - SOA, and integrated information infrastructure) and universal data models and standard data structures emerge, integration toward the high end of the spectrum will be facilitated. However, there will always be the need for effective standards governance to reduce the need for manual co-ordination and conflict resolution.

Explanation :

---

49. https://pubs.opengroup.org/togaf-standard/adm/chap01.html#tagfcjh_3

See : **1.7 Architecture Integration**[50] under Architecture Development Method part of TOGAF® Standard Fundamental Content Version 10

Figure 1-3[51] illustrates how different types of architecture **need to co-exist**.

Answer : B

50. https://pubs.opengroup.org/togaf-standard/adm/chap01.html#tag_01_07

51. https://pubs.opengroup.org/togaf-standard/adm/chap01.html#tagfcjh_3

Module 11 : Architecture Repository

Note that questions do come up with answer choices and correct answer picked up from other modules beyond these. Revisit all questions after revising the whole of TOGAF®.

Cross References shown as 'See' herein refer to : **7. Architecture Repository**[1] under Architecture Content part of TOGAF® Standard Fundamental Content Version 10

In case any other free-standing document of TOGAF® Standard Fundamental Content Version 10 or Series Guide is referenced, that is explicitly mentioned.

Q 1101 Which of the following lists the components within the Architecture Repository ?

A. Organizational Metamodel, Architecture Capability, Architecture Landscape, Best Practices, Reference Library, Compliance Strategy

B. Architecture Metamodel, Organizational Capability Model, Application Landscape, SIB, Reference Library, Governance Model

C. Business Metamodel, Architecture Capability, Architecture Landscape, SIB, Reference Library, Governance Repository

D. Architecture Metamodel, Architecture Capability, Architecture Landscape, SIB, Reference Library, Governance Repository

Explanation :

It is important to get to know the names of each of the six sections as also about the nature of contents stored therein. Note that this is the Repository of Architectural contents for the whole Enterprise. So it will be a comprehensive one accommodating a variety of assets.

See Under : **7.1 Overview**[2] : At a high level, the following classes of architectural information are expected to be held within an Architecture Repository :

▪ The **Architecture Metamodel** describes the .... of an architecture framework, including a .... and a metamodel for ....content : Tailored TOGAF® - note how ADM duly customized is also mentioned specifically here, plus tailored Content Metamodel as customized : What artifacts and Building Blocks to be prepared under each Phase, what is the metamodel definition of each artifact therein. (For advanced treatment of this, do see : **Chapter 2. TOGAF Content Framework and Enterprise Metamodel**[3]

▪ The **Architecture Capability** defines the ...., ..., and ... that support .... Repository : Practice guidelines to EA team that will strengthen proper conducting of their work and thus further the governance system. Parameters – what are needed, Structures – in what organized form, process – in what order of execution the best practices are to be understood and

---

1. https://pubs.opengroup.org/togaf-standard/architecture-content/chap07.html

2. https://pubs.opengroup.org/togaf-standard/architecture-content/chap07.html#tag_07_01

3. https://pubs.opengroup.org/togaf-standard/architecture-content/chap02.html

practiced. Specific reference to' governance of the Architecture Repository' appears since all such guidelines are meant to improve the governance process and do end up stored in the Architecture Repository itself.

▪ The **Architecture Landscape** presents an .... of assets ..., or ..., by the .. points in time : All artifact Building Blocks and all deliverables prepared by us from all earlier project portfolios till current ones are stored here so that they are available for reference and re-use. In use – means, already approved and have been implemented. Planned – means, under finalization for current portfolios 'in-flight'.

▪ The **Standards Information Base** captures the ...with which ... must comply, which may include ...., selected ... and ... from suppliers, or shared services ... : See all that are mentioned here. These ones, which are needed in our portfolios (earlier or now) for look-up first and then compliance next are stored in this section.

▪ The **Reference Library** provides ..., ..., ..., and other forms of reference material that can ... in order to accelerate the ... for the enterprise : Usually third party references such as Foundational Architectures, Common System Architectures, Industry specific reference materials relevant to the vertical of the Enterprise, Patterns of various nature and a wide spread of it, Software Architecture and Software Engineering guidelines needed to educate and inform the architects (and developers) are templates thereof stored here. Sometime POC - Proof Of Concept architectures and architectural output of centre of Excellence can also be placed here.

▪ The **Governance Repository** provides a record of .... across the enterprise : All that has happened and which is of interest to those in the Governance activity – ideally for the Architecture Governance Board and those higher officials in EA department who govern others in the department. Log means recorded information of what transpired, what happened till now. Note that in TOGAF® 10, this section is renamed as Governance Repository.

Note : Refer to **Figure 7-1 : Overview of Architecture Repository and read the following**[4] :

Architecture Metamodel : Not only the tailored TOGAF®, but an Enterprise (Content) Metamodel[5]

The two other sections appearing in the figure above are :

Architecture Requirements Repository : only in-flight, Work in progress. Of those project architecture requirements which are in suitably approved Statement of Architecture Work

Solutions Landscape : All which have been planned (in-flight) or deployed (implemented as existing projects). Still it is the SBBs (often called as Design Store) and is not a repository of codes and executables, which are to be maintained by the PMO and not the EA department.

Answer : D

––––––––––––––

Q 1102 Which one of the following does TOGAF® recommend be created to address integration of individual architectures ?

A. An Architecture Repository

B. An Enterprise Continuum

---

4. **https://pubs.opengroup.org/togaf-standard/architecture-content/chap07.html#tagfcjh_16**

5. https://pubs.opengroup.org/togaf-standard/architecture-content/chap02.html

C. An Integrated Information Infrastructure Reference Model

D. A meta-architecture framework

E. A technical reference model

Explanation :

TOGAF® recommends meta-architecture framework in this case. The integrated changes can be stored in Architecture Metamodel portion of the Architecture Repository.

A meta-architecture is one that describes how a specific architecture is to be performed. To this extent the TOGAF® Documentation taken as it is or the same duly tailored for an Enterprise all fall under the category of meta-architecture.

As an Enterprise Architecture framework, we know that the TOGAF® framework provides a basis for developing architectures in a uniform and consistent manner. Its purpose in this respect is to ensure that the various Architecture Descriptions developed within an Enterprise, perhaps by different architects or architecture teams, support the comparison and integration of architectures within and across architecture domains (Business, Data, Application, Technology), and relating to different business area scopes within the Enterprise.

7.1 Overview[6]

The **Architecture Metamodel** describes ... tailored .. architecture framework, including.... a .. and a ... content

Note that the 'method for architecture development' refers to ADM in the way it is **tailored for the Enterprise**[7]. Also note that the 'metamodel for architecture content' refers to the **Content Framework and Enterprise Metamodel**[8]

Answer : D

─────────────

Q 1103 A list of Capabilities as considered under Enterprise Architecture may not include

A. Architecture Value

B. Architecture Planning

C. Architecture Framework

D. Architecture Processes

E. Unit Test Results

Explanation :

See : **2.1 Overview**[9] : 2. Establishing an Architecture Capability : Enterprise Architecture Capability and Governance part of TOGAF® Standard Fundamental Content Version 10

---

6. https://pubs.opengroup.org/togaf-standard/architecture-content/chap07.html#tag_07_01

7. https://pubs.opengroup.org/togaf-standard/adm/chap02.html#tag_02_03_05

8. https://pubs.opengroup.org/togaf-standard/architecture-content/chap02.html#tag_02_01

9. https://pubs.opengroup.org/togaf-standard/ea-capability-and-governance/chap02.html#tag_02_01

As with any business capability, ... can be supported by ... (ADM).

Successful use of the ...will provide a ...., ..., and ... that enables the ..., helps ... of investments, and pro-actively identifies ... to gain business ... and manage ...: Read about how ADM contributes to this aspect. This is important.

On incorrect answer choices :

Answer choice A) : Architecture Value : Not a capability. Just a measure.

Answer choice B) : Architecture Planning : Not a capability. It is an action.

Answer choice C) : Architecture Framework : May contain guidelines and process for Architecture Capability. Just as TOGAF® has Part VI: Architecture Capability Framework.

Answer choice D) : Unit Test Results : Not a capability. Just a result of verification.

Answer : E

Q 1104 What part of the Architecture Repository shows the Building Blocks that are currently in use within the organization ?

A. Architecture Landscape

B. Architecture Metamodel

C. Governance Repository

D. Reference Library

E. Standards Information Base

Explanation :

Landscape is to contain : Building Blocks, comprising of ABB and SBB assets which have been prepared earlier for IT projects which are currently executing. Also the ADM outputs of projects currently in ADM phases and which are approved by EA. These will be stored in the Architectural Landscape of the Repository, duly channelized by the Content Framework as a Schema.

Note Again : under Section **3.11 Architecture Repository**[10] : 3. Core Concepts under Introduction and Core Concepts part of TOGAF® Standard Fundamental Content Version 10

The **Architecture Landscape** is the ... of assets deployed ... at a ... — the landscape is likely to exist at ... to suit ...

Note that **Figure 3-1**[11] shows a summary of the classification model for Architecture Landscapes.

See **3. Applying the ADM Across the Architecture Landscape**[12] under Applying the ADM part of TOGAF® Standard Fundamental Content Version 10

---

10. https://pubs.opengroup.org/togaf-standard/introduction/chap03.html#tag_03_11

11. https://pubs.opengroup.org/togaf-standard/applying-the-adm/chap03.html#tagfcjh_6

Architecture Landscape : Levels provide ... into three levels of granularity :

1. **Strategic Architecture** provides ...

1. **Segment Architecture** provides ...

1. **Capability Architecture** provides ...

Read explanation appearing under **Q 1001**

Answer : A

———————

Q 1105 A standard is different from other Reference Models because

A. Standard is something to be complied with, while Reference Models can be adapted to suit the Enterprise

B. Standards are made in house while Reference Models are obtained from external sources

C. Standards are obtained from external sources while Reference Models are made in house

D. None of the above are reasons for the difference

Explanation :

By basic definition, Standards are issued so that the Architecture work is prepared in compliance with it. These are often issued by standard bodies and neutral bodies.

Reference Models, mostly coming from third party outside the Enterprise could not be exactly incorporated into the practices and technologies that are considered. Hence, they may be examined, adapted and customized (if so needed) before being placed in the Repository of the Enterprise.

See : **4.63 Reference Model (RM)**[13] : 4. Definitions under Introduction and Core Concepts part of TOGAF® Standard Fundamental Content Version 10

An abstract framework ..., and for ....: Mentioned as an 'abstract framework' since they may have to studied, adapted to suit the situation of need. Abstract because they could be generic and not to specific and for exact situation. Framework because it is not 'do exactly like this' kind of commands but a general 'frame' that needs study and adaptation. (**Note that even TOGAF® as a whole is known as a 'generic and abstract framework' for similar reasons. It may need heavy customization and tailoring before it is accepted as highly practical.**)

A reference model is based on .... : What is the basis of a reference model ? What are the things it is not directly tied to and what are the things it seeks to provide ?

A reference model is not ..., but it does seek ..

---

12. https://pubs.opengroup.org/togaf-standard/applying-the-adm/chap03.html#tag_03

13. https://pubs.opengroup.org/togaf-standard/introduction/chap04.html#tag_04_63

Also note from above that Reference model by itself may be abstract and we need to adopt it for the Enterprise. This is done for the first time in Preliminary Phase and is subjected to additions during ADM, if at all necessary

See under **3.6.6 Phase D : Technology Architecture : Technology Portfolio Catalog**[14] : 3. Architectural Artifacts under Architecture Content part of TOGAF® Standard Fundamental Content Version 10

If technology standards are currently in place, apply these to the Technology Portfolio catalog to gain a baseline view of compliance with technology standards.

See : **7.4 Standards Library**[15]

The Standards Library provides ..., to which architectures ....

7.4.2 Types of Standard

- Legal and Regulatory Obligations : ... must comply or ..
- Industry Standards : these standards are ..., and are then selected .. for adoption
- Organizational Standards : these standards are set .. and are based on ..
-

7.4.3 Standards Lifecycle

Standards do not ... New standards are .. a lifecycle process.

7.4.4 Standards Classification within the Standards Library

- Business Standards : ....
- Data Standards : .....
- Applications Standards : .....
- Technology Standards : ...

Answer : A

———————————

Q 1106 Which component of the Architecture Repository provides guidelines, templates, and patterns that can be used to create new architectures ?

A. The Architecture Metamodel

B. The Architecture Capability

C. The Architecture Landscape

D. The Reference Library

E. The Governance Repository

---

14. https://pubs.opengroup.org/togaf-standard/architecture-content/chap03.html#tag_03_06_06_02

15. https://pubs.opengroup.org/togaf-standard/architecture-content/chap07.html#tag_07_04

Explanation :

The very purpose of Reference Library is to store those materials which could be referenced by Architects from time to time. It is natural that such content is in the form of guideline materials, template suggestions and patterns and many more useful references like these which pertain to best practices.

See : **7.1 : The Reference Library**[16] provides ..., and other forms of .. that can be leveraged ..

Also see : **7.3.1 Overview**[17]

The Reference Library provides ... that should be used to ...

Reference materials .., including :

▪ ... bodies ▪ ... vendors ▪ ...communities or forums

▪ ... templates ▪ ...best practice

The Reference Library should contain :

▪ ... Architectures ▪ ... Models ▪ ... Library

▪ ....

These are at **7. Architecture Repository**[18] under Architecture Content part of TOGAF® Standard Fundamental Content Version 10

Read the relevant portion about this from the explanation appearing under **Q 1101**

Answer : D

———————————

Q 1107 Statement that is true with Governance Repository

A. Contains a record of what happened as part of governance activity across the enterprise

B. Tailored Governance processes

C. Capability improvement process under Governance

D. Standards referred to as part of governance and Regulation

Explanation :

As the name implies, it is only a 'log record' of what has happened.

See : **7.5.1 : The Governance Repository**[19] provides a ... across the enterprise.

16. https://pubs.opengroup.org/togaf-standard/architecture-content/chap07.html#tag_07_03

17. https://pubs.opengroup.org/togaf-standard/architecture-content/chap07.html#tag_07_03_01

18. https://pubs.opengroup.org/togaf-standard/architecture-content/chap07.html

19. https://pubs.opengroup.org/togaf-standard/architecture-content/chap07.html#tag_07_05_01

The Governance Repository provides .. to hold shared information relating to ....

Maintaining ... is important, because:

- ... during ...

For example, ...

- Many stakeholders are interested in the ...

Also See : **7.5.2 Contents of the Governance Repository**[20]

decisions made by the Governance authorities, including dispensations after Architecture Compliance Review.

▪ **Compliance Assessments :** at key .... in the progress of a ..., a formal ...w will be carried out : Details of Architecture Compliance Review at mid-points and endpoint of a portfolio or project.

▪ **Capability Assessments :** depending on their ...., some projects will carry out ... Capability : Architecture Capability Maturity Assessment, made as a dedicated assignment (say in Preliminary Phase) or as part of any other project. Can also be only for Business Capability or for IT Capability.

▪ **Calendar :** the Calendar should show a schedule of ..... and formal ... to be held against these .. : Currently on-going projects or portfolios, a schedule of events on when review sessions are to be held.

▪ **Project Portfolio :** the Project Portfolio should hold ... about all ... that fall under Architecture .... : Summary details on architectural aspects of currently on-going projects and portfolios.

▪ **Performance Measurement :** based on a .... for the ...., a number of ... will typically .... : Criterion such as SLA – Service Level Agreement and other important metrics on such performance measurement aspects.

Explanation of why other choices are not the answer :

Tailored Governance process, or for that matter any Tailored TOGAF® will be part of Architecture Meta Model. This model will contain Tailored and non-tailored (in case no customization is done) TOGAF® standard serving as a meta documentation.

All Capability related concepts and processes will be part of Architecture Capability.

All standards, which are mostly made by others, as well as a few which are internally prepare standards should be ideally part of SIB.

Read the relevant portion about this from the explanation appearing under **Q 1101**

Answer : A

Note : If you are seeing this as 'Governance Log' instead of as 'Governance Repository', then you are referring to wrong specification which is not TOGAF® 10. Please stop referring to it. In TOGAF® 10, this is known as Governance Repository only.

---

20. https://pubs.opengroup.org/togaf-standard/architecture-content/chap07.html#tag_07_05_02

Q 1108 Which of the following is organizationally tailored application of an architecture framework which includes method for architecture development and metamodel for architecture content ?

A. Architecture Capability

B. Architecture Landscape

C. Standards Information Bas

D. Architecture Metamodel

Explanation :

Metamodel refers to any definition of how a model should be. TOGAF® documentation is considered to be a definition of models (including ADM, Frameworks therein). It is recommended to be tailored before being placed in the Architecture Repository as a content.

TOGAF® documentation is considered to be a definition of models (including ADM, Frameworks therein). The content model is seen in **Chapter : 2. TOGAF® Content Framework and Enterprise Metamodel**[21]

See : **7.1 : The Architecture Metamodel**[22] describes the ..., including .. and a ....

Note the step in Preliminary Phase : **Step 2.3.5**[23] : 2. Preliminary Phase under Architecture Development Method part of TOGAF® Standard Fundamental Content Version 10

Tailor the ... and, if any, ..

After such a Tailoring, the Metamodel (the model that describes how to model and architecture EA as per adapted TOGAF® – The Tailored TOGAF®, known here as Architecture Method) is placed in the Architecture Repository.

Note : For the Enterprise Metamodel portion, refer to : **2. TOGAF® Content Framework and Enterprise Metamodel**[24] under Architecture Content part of TOGAF® Standard Fundamental Content Version 10

The purpose of the TOGAF® framework is to provide an open standard for architecture. This should remain true for different many scenarios and situations that occur in the Enterprise.

While moving towards such a vision, we need to have a fully featured Enterprise Architecture metamodel. This metamodel should cover the content list and definition. It should also have the ability to steering away from activities that are not relevant. Hence we go for the tailoring of not just the TOGAF® Framework, but also its metamodel.

The metamodel is expected to provide a model of the very basics, having the minimum feature set. It can still accommodate optional extensions during the tailoring exercise.

Answer : D

_____

---

21. https://pubs.opengroup.org/togaf-standard/architecture-content/chap02.html#tag_02

22. https://pubs.opengroup.org/togaf-standard/architecture-content/chap07.html#tag_07_01

23. https://pubs.opengroup.org/togaf-standard/adm/chap02.html#tag_02_03_05

24. https://pubs.opengroup.org/togaf-standard/architecture-content/chap02.html#tag_02

Q 1109 A list of those defined by Architecture Capability to support the governance of the Architecture Repository includes

A. Parameters

B. Structure

C. Processes

D. None of the above

E. All of the (first three) above

Explanation :

It is parameters, structures, and processes that support governance of the Architecture Repository.

See under : **7.1 :**[25] **The Architecture Capability** defines the ... that support governance of the Architecture Repository.

When it says that this in in 'support governance of the Architecture Repository', it should ideally mean all best practice guidelines that is followed in ADM during which the Architecture repository is either populated of referred to.

This Architecture **Repository is one part** of the wider Enterprise Repository, which provides the capability to link architectural assets to components of the Detailed Design, Deployment, and Service Management Repositories.

Also note from : **3.1.1 Levels of Governance within the Enterprise**[26] : Enterprise Architecture Capability and Governance part of TOGAF® Standard Fundamental Content Version 10

Architecture Governance is the ... by which ... are managed and controlled ....

Further note from : **3.2.1.2 Key Architecture Governance Processes**[27] : **Environment Management** : Enterprise Architecture Capability and Governance part of TOGAF® Standard Fundamental Content Version 10

This identifies all the .. to ensure that the ... is ....

This includes the ....

Answer : E

Q 1110 Complete the sentence. The Architecture Landscape is divided into three levels, Strategic, Segment and _____.

A. Baseline

B. Capability

C. Solution

25. https://pubs.opengroup.org/togaf-standard/architecture-content/chap07.html#tag_07_01

26. https://pubs.opengroup.org/togaf-standard/ea-capability-and-governance/chap03.html#tag_03_01_01

27. https://pubs.opengroup.org/togaf-standard/ea-capability-and-governance/chap03.html#tag_03_02_01_02

D. Target

E. Transition

Explanation :

Strategic (long term initiatives), Segment (portfolio level taken up in the medium term, as a tactical move) and Capability (Transition Architectures of immediate value) are the **three partitions** of Architecture Landscape.

See under : **7.2 Architecture Landscape**[28] : The Architecture Landscape holds ... in time.

Due to the ..., the Architecture Landscape is divided into ... :

1. **Strategic Architectures** .... Strategic Architectures provide ...for ... and allow for ...

1. **Segment Architectures** .... Segment Architectures can be used ... to ...

1. **Capability Architectures** show in a more detailed fashion how .... Capability Architectures are used ...and allow for ..

Such a feature of partition supports the developing architecture for different purposes, or levels of detail, and thus can be applied to support Agile software development

Read explanation appearing under **Q 1001**

Answer : B

———————

ALSO NOTE FROM : **12.1 Architecture in an Agile Enterprise**[29] in TOGAF® Series Guide : A Practitioners' Approach to Developing Enterprise Architecture Following the TOGAF® ADM

There has been .. about aligning to ...

Ink has been spilled trying to .. to these ...

The TOGAF® Standard aligns to agile development in ...

A good Architecture to ..., will identify ...

In short, a good architecture defines ....

Architecture to ... will have a set of ....

These constraints are .. and the ...

... Phase G, Implementation Governance : the Practitioner ....

In short, guarding ....

---

28. https://pubs.opengroup.org/togaf-standard/architecture-content/chap07.html#tag_07_02

29. https://pubs.opengroup.org/togaf-standard/adm-practitioners/adm-practitioners_12.html#_Toc95288909

Note : Questions do come up from Series Guides, especially from portions mentioned in the Exam syllabus. This Series of Books have incorporated such references at the appropriate places. Please do not ignore them.

Q 1111 What level of the Architecture Landscape provides a long-term summary view of the entire enterprise ?

A. Capability Architecture

B. Operational Architecture

C. Segment Architecture

D. Strategic Architecture

E. Tactical Architecture

Explanation :

Strategic Architecture always looks at a long-term view of the Enterprise and is about thinking of Initiatives and Goals to relieve the pain points faced by the Enterprise and to improve the overall Architectural maturity through more innovative and modern means.

See under : **7.2 Architecture Landscape**[30] : **Strategic Architectures** show .... Strategic Architectures provide ... and allow for ...

Strategic Architecture is the one that provide a comprehensive and omnibus view of entire Enterprise.

Strategic Architecture provides an organizing framework for ...

Also see : **Figure 3-1 Summary Classification Model for Architecture Landscapes**[31]

These are at **3. Applying the ADM Across the Architecture Landscape**[32] under Applying the ADM part of TOGAF® Standard Fundamental Content Version 10

Read explanation appearing under **Q 1001**

Answer : D

Q 1112 Which class of architectural information held within the Architecture Repository would contain adapted reference models ?

A. Architecture Metamodel

B. Architecture Capability

C. Standards Information Base

---

30. https://pubs.opengroup.org/togaf-standard/architecture-content/chap07.html#tag_07_02

31. https://pubs.opengroup.org/togaf-standard/applying-the-adm/chap03.html#tagfcjh_6

32. https://pubs.opengroup.org/togaf-standard/applying-the-adm/chap03.html#tag_03

D. Reference Library

Explanation :

TOGAF® asks us not just to store reference materials of architecture importance as it is, but will expect us to adopt it (make changes to suit our need, add comments and so on) while it is being stored.

See under : **7.3.1 : Overview : Reference Library**[33]

Typically, a generic reference architecture provides ... with an .. that will be ....

This customisation leads to ....

These are ideally identified upfront .. and placed in the ..

Also see : **4.86 Viewpoint Library**[34] : **4. Definitions** under Introduction and Core Concepts part of TOGAF® Standard Fundamental Content Version 10

A collection of the ...

We have "Industry Architectures", in terms of the Enterprise Continuum. They are held in the Reference Library of the Architecture Repository.

Answer : D

————————

Q 1113 Which of the following applies to Reference Library in a TOGAF® Architecture Repository ?

A. Define parameters, structures and processes that governs the Architecture Repository

B. Standards that new architectures should comply

C. Guidelines, templates, patterns and other forms of material which can be used to accelerate the development of new architecture

D. Record of governance activity for the enterprise

Explanation :

Reference Library is full of guidelines, templates, patterns and many other forms of reference material. These are meant to be used by the EA Team to accelerate the development of the architecture under current ADM cycle.

See under : **7.1 : Overview : Architecture Repository**[35] : The **Reference Library** provides ..., and other forms of .. that can be ..

Also note from : **2.3 The TOGAF® Library**[36] : **2. The TOGAF® Documentation Set** : under Introduction and Core Concepts part of TOGAF® Standard Fundamental Content Version 10

33. https://pubs.opengroup.org/togaf-standard/architecture-content/chap07.html#tag_07_01

34. https://pubs.opengroup.org/togaf-standard/introduction/chap04.html#tag_04_86

35. https://pubs.opengroup.org/togaf-standard/architecture-content/chap07.html#tag_07_01

Accompanying this standard is ..., known as the ..., to support the ...

The ... is a reference library containing ....

The ... supports ..., the Reference Library.

The Reference Library provides ...

The ... is a Reference Library of ....

The ... follows a ... based on ... that can be ... through ....

Answer : C

─────────────

Q 1114 What is the process of defining parameters, structures and processes that governs the Architecture Repository ?

A. Reference Library

B. Standard Information Base

C. Architecture Capability

D. Architecture Meta Model

Explanation :

Architecture Repository itself requires a defined process of its parameters and structures. This is found in the Architecture Capability section of itself.

See under : **7.1**[37]

The **Architecture Capability** defines ... that support ....

This Architecture Repository is one part of the wider Enterprise Repository.

Also note from : **3.1.1 Levels of Governance within the Enterprise**[38] : Enterprise Architecture Capability and Governance part of TOGAF® Standard Fundamental Content Version 10

Architecture Governance is the ...by which ... are ....

Further note from : **3.2.1.2 Key Architecture Governance Processes**[39] : **Environment Management** : Enterprise Architecture Capability and Governance part of TOGAF® Standard Fundamental Content Version 10

This identifies all the ... to ensure that the ... underpinning the .... is effective and efficient. This includes the .... and ..., ..., ..., ... and a... of all users : The environment of governance is placed around the Architecture Repository. It has to

─────────────

36. https://pubs.opengroup.org/togaf-standard/introduction/chap02.html#tag_02_03

37. https://pubs.opengroup.org/togaf-standard/architecture-content/chap07.html#tag_07_01

38. https://pubs.opengroup.org/togaf-standard/ea-capability-and-governance/chap03.html#tag_03_01_01

39. https://pubs.opengroup.org/togaf-standard/ea-capability-and-governance/chap03.html#tag_03_02_01_02

ensure proper access for the users and adequate communication with them. Also involves providing right kind of skills training, and due accreditation of the users.

All ....artifacts, service ...., and .... information must come under ... through a ... in order to ... and ...new or updated content. These processes will ensure the .... with ... such that all ... are managed and audited : The environment of governance, which is seen all around the Repository is directly connected with architectural artifacts, service agreements, and all related supporting information. The content related tasks are much beyond mere registering the category of the artifact but extends right into validation and approval and subsequent management of content through publishing activities, as also through periodical updates. It will tie itself back to existing governance practices and even an audit thereon.

The governance environment will have .... defined in order to .... and ..... These processes will include ..., ... (defined ... processes), and .... reporting : Note how the governance environment has its influence on post architectural activities of managed services and user management, maintaining a management information system and so on. This is why the Repository and its Architecture Capability section is tied down to many of governance activities and the best practices advocated thereon.

Answer : C

_____

Q 1115 What part of the Architecture Repository holds specifications to which architectures must conform ?

A. Standards Information Base

B. Enterprise Continuum

C. Governance Repository

D. Architecture Landscape

E. Reference Library

Explanation :

Standards are the ones which every part of the architecture must comply. Standards Information Base, SIB, is the area in the Architecture Repository where standards are stored.

See under : **7.1**[40] : The **Standards Information Base** captures ,, with which ..., which may ...

See : **7.4.1 Overview**[41] : The Standards Information Base provides ..., to which ... : What holds what ?

Establishment of a Standards Information Base provides .. for ... because :

▪ The standards are ...

▪ Standards are ..., so that ...

So, Standards compliance is used as part of .... .. unambiguous basis for architectural governance.

---

40. https://pubs.opengroup.org/togaf-standard/architecture-content/chap07.html#tag_07_01

41. https://pubs.opengroup.org/togaf-standard/architecture-content/chap07.html#tag_07_04_01

Also note that the types of standards, all of which aid the Governance process : **7.4.2 Types of Standard**[42]

▪ **Legal and Regulatory Obligations :** these standards are ...

▪ **Industry Standards:** these standards are ...

▪ **Organizational Standards:** these standards are ...

Answer : A

––––––––––––––

Q 1116 Which one of the following statements is correct in the context of ADM and Architecture Repository relationship ?

A. At relevant places throughout the ADM, there are reminders to consider which architecture assets from the Architecture Repository the architect should use

B. The practical implementation of the Enterprise Continuum will typically take the form of an Architecture Repository that includes reference architectures, models, and patterns mandated in TOGAF®

C. In executing the ADM, the architect is only developing a snapshot of the enterprise at particular points in time, and populating the organization's own Architecture Repository is outside the scope of ADM

D. The first execution of the ADM is simplified because of the re-use potential of the standard architecture assets available for re-use in TOGAF® Architecture Repository

E. Architecture Repository is only accessed in the Requirement Management Phase

Explanation :

Looking at the incorrect answer choices

The practical implementation of the Enterprise Continuum will typically take the form of an Architecture Repository that includes reference architectures, models, and patterns mandated in TOGAF® – **Not a ADM and Architecture Repository relationship**; read this question again after you get to know about Enterprise Continuum.

In executing the ADM, the architect is only developing a snapshot of the Enterprise at particular points in time, and populating the organization's own Architecture Repository is outside the scope of ADM – **ADM goes through actions which are much more than a snapshot of the Enterprise.** ADM populates the Architecture Repository with Architectures that are Platform independent (ABBs), Solutions which are implementation and vendor biased (Platform Specific SBBs) and even Implementation Governance and Change Management records thereafter.

The first execution of the ADM is simplified because of the re-use potential of the standard architecture assets available for re-use in TOGAF® Architecture Repository - **Not a point relevant** to ADM and Architecture Repository relationship. In fact the first execution will be tougher due to lack of content in the Architecture Landscape.

Architecture Repository is only accessed in the Requirement Management phase – **Totally wrong** understanding of ADM phases including its Requirement Management Phase.

––

42. https://pubs.opengroup.org/togaf-standard/architecture-content/chap07.html#tag_07_04_02

Answer : A

Also **note from** : **5.1 What to Expect in a Well-Run Architecture Repository**[43] : TOGAF® Series Guide : A Practitioners' Approach to Developing Enterprise Architecture Following the TOGAF® ADM

―――――――

Q 1117 Which of the following acts as a holding area for all architecture related projects within the enterprise ?

A. Architecture Building Block

B. Architecture Repository

C. Architecture Roadmap

D. Architecture Vision

Explanation :

Architecture Repository is the one that acts as a holding area for all architecture related projects within the Enterprise.

See under : **7.1**[44] The **Architecture Landscape** presents an ... of assets .., or .., by the ....

Do not forget that the Architecture Landscape is one among the six major constituents of the Architecture Repository.

Quoting from TOGAF® documentation on incorrect Answer Choices :

Answer Choice A) Architecture Building Block : **3.6 Deliverables, Artifacts, and Building Blocks**[45] under Introduction and Core Concepts part of TOGAF® Standard Fundamental Content Version 10

Architecture Building Blocks (ABBs) typically describe ...; for example, a ..., supported by many SBBs, such as ....

Answer Choice C) Architecture Roadmap : **4.65 Roadmap**[46] : **4. Definitions** under Introduction and Core Concepts part of TOGAF® Standard Fundamental Content Version 10

An abstracted plan for ..., typically operating across ... over ....

Normally used in the phrases ...., etc., : Important definitions. See how it is used in related phrases as mentioned here.

Answer Choice D) Architecture Vision : **4.22 Architecture Vision**[47] : **4. Definitions** under Introduction and Core Concepts part of TOGAF® Standard Fundamental Content Version 10 : What kind of description ? What does it describe ?

A succinct description of the .. that describes ... and the ... that will ....

It serves as an ... and a boundary for ....

43. https://pubs.opengroup.org/togaf-standard/adm-practitioners/adm-practitioners_5.html#_Toc95288826

44. https://pubs.opengroup.org/togaf-standard/architecture-content/chap07.html#tag_07_01

45. https://pubs.opengroup.org/togaf-standard/introduction/chap03.html#tag_03_06

46. https://pubs.opengroup.org/togaf-standard/introduction/chap04.html#tag_04_65

47. https://pubs.opengroup.org/togaf-standard/introduction/chap04.html#tag_04_22

Answer : B

———————————

Q 1118 Which component within the Architecture Repository holds best practice or template materials that can be used to construct architectures ?

A. Architecture Capability

B. Architecture Landscape

C. Architecture Metamodel

D. Governance Repository

E. Reference Library

Explanation :

Reference Library is the one that holds best practice or template materials that can be used to construct further architectures.

See under : **7.1**[48] : The **Reference Library** provides ... that can be leveraged in order to ....

Patterns and other forms of reference materials are brought in by EA (in Preliminary Phase itself) to be of value as Best Practices. The very purpose of Reference Library is to hold and store the content which is often referenced by Architects as and when they need it. It is natural that such content is in the form of guideline materials, template suggestions and patterns that pertain to best practices.

Also see : **7.3.1 : Overview**[49] : The Reference Library provides ...to develop architectures.

Reference materials ... sources, including :

- ...bodies ▪ .... vendors ▪ ...communities or forums

- ... Standard templates ▪ .. best practice

The Reference Library should contain :

- ..Architectures ▪ ... Models ▪ ....Library

- ....

Read the relevant portion about this from the explanation appearing under **Q 1101 and Q 903**

Answer : E

———————————

48. https://pubs.opengroup.org/togaf-standard/architecture-content/chap07.html#tag_07_01

49. https://pubs.opengroup.org/togaf-standard/architecture-content/chap07.html#tag_07_03_01

Q 1119 Which one of the following completes the sentence : When executing the ADM, the architect is not only developing a snapshot of the enterprise, but is also populating the _____

A. Architecture Repository

B. Architecture Capability Framework

C. Enterprise Continuum

D. Foundation Architecture

Explanation :

Architect is producing artifacts which is populated (stored) in the Architecture Repository. The Architecture Capability Framework is a set of best practices and guidelines and not a model that is populated as such. Actually this Architecture Capability Framework is only improved with higher capability.

See : **1.1.1 The ADM, Enterprise Continuum, and Architecture Repository**[50] : 1. Introduction under Architecture Development Method part of TOGAF® Standard Fundamental Content Version 10: What all does it provide, to support what ? What are the assets mentioned here ?

The .... provides a framework and context to ... in executing the ADM.

These assets may include ....

The practical implementation of the... will typically take the ...that includes ... that have been ... and actual .... : Note the way the two important Components of TOGAF® are related. What is mentioned here about re-use and what is the mention there about currently in progress projects ?

The .. seek to ... from the ... that was ....

(In addition to the ..., the ... also contain ...).

Also see : **1.1.2 The ADM and the Foundation Architecture Repository**[51] : 1. Introduction under Architecture Development Method part of TOGAF® Standard Fundamental Content Version 10: Points to note, regarding how Foundation architectures are populated.

The ADM is also useful ... of an ...

Business requirements ... may be used to identify the .. in the ...

This could be a ... or even as ....

Population of the ... follows ..., with the difference that ... and thus ....

Answer : A

---

50. https://pubs.opengroup.org/togaf-standard/adm/chap01.html#tag_01_01_01

51. https://pubs.opengroup.org/togaf-standard/adm/chap01.html#tag_01_01_02

Q 1120 When applying a cycle of the ADM with the Architecture Vision to establish an Architecture Capability, which phase does TOGAF® recommends as that which defines the structure of the organization's Architecture Repository ?

A. Application Architecture

B. Business Architecture

C. Data Architecture

D. Preliminary Phase

E. Technology Architecture

Explanation :

The Data Architecture would define the structure of the organization's Enterprise Continuum and Architecture Repository. In other words, the Data Architect will draw up the architecture towards this Repository.

See : **2.4 Phase C : Data Architecture**[52] : 2. Establishing an Architecture Capability : Enterprise Architecture Capability and Governance part of TOGAF® Standard Fundamental Content Version 10

The Data Architecture ... would ... the ... and ...

The Data Architecture should be ....

The ... is sometimes referred to as the metamodel of the architecture practice.....

Also see : **2.1 Overview (Establishing an Architecture Capability)**[53] : 2. Establishing an Architecture Capability : Enterprise Architecture Capability and Governance part of TOGAF® Standard Fundamental Content Version 10

Implementing ... within an organization would require ...: ....

Establishing the ... within .. would therefore require .. :

▪ The **Data Architecture** that would ..

▪ The **Technology Architecture** that ... and deployment in support of the ...

Answer : C

――――――――――

Q 1121 Which of the following best completes the sentence ? The Architecture Repository _____.

A. is used to store different classes of architectural output created by the ADM or needed by the ADM

B. is a categorization mechanism for classifying architecture and solution artifacts

C. is a detailed model of architectural work products, including deliverables and artifacts

―――――――――――――――――――――――――――――――――――――――

52. https://pubs.opengroup.org/togaf-standard/ea-capability-and-governance/chap02.html#tag_02_04

53. https://pubs.opengroup.org/togaf-standard/ea-capability-and-governance/chap02.html#tag_02_01

D. is an architecture of generic functions and services

E. is a set of resources to help establish an architecture capability within an organization

Explanation :

Architecture Repository which can be used to store different classes of architectural output at different levels of abstraction - ABBs created in the process of ADM.

See under : **3.11 : Architecture Repository**[54] : Core Concepts under Introduction and Core Concepts part of TOGAF® Standard Fundamental Content Version 10

Supporting the ... is the concept of an ... which can be used to ... at different ..., created by ...

In this way, the TOGAF® Standard facilitates ... between .. at ..

On non-correct Answer Choices :

Enterprise Continuum categorization mechanism for classifying architecture and solution artifacts

Content Meta Model and Content Framework : These have a detailed model of architectural work products, including deliverables and artifacts

Foundation Architecture (and TRM) is an architecture of generic functions and services

ADM and its guidelines are a set of resources to help establish an architecture capability within an organization

Answer : A

Q 1122 Complete the sentence. The ADM can be viewed as the process of populating the enterprise's own _____ with relevant re-usable Building Blocks taken from the more generic side of the Enterprise Continuum.

A. Architecture Repository

B. Architecture Requirements

C. Implementation and Migration plan

D. Standards Information Base

E. Strategic Architecture

Explanation :

ADM is a process that populates the Architecture Repository. When seen from a wider perspective, it is also populating relevant re-usable Building Blocks taken from the more generic side of the Enterprise Continuum.

See : **1.1.1 The ADM, Enterprise Continuum, and Architecture Repository**[55] : 1. Introduction under Architecture Development Method part of TOGAF® Standard Fundamental Content Version 10

---

54. https://pubs.opengroup.org/togaf-standard/introduction/chap03.html#tag_03_11

Architecture development is a .... process, and in executing the ... time, the architect ... organization's Architecture Repository : Read here about content addition.

Although the primary focus of the ADM is on the .... architecture, in this wider context the ADM can .... as the process of .... own Architecture ... with relevant ... taken from the ".....", more .... of the Enterprise Continuum : What to see in the wider context ? What is the left side mentioned here and what happens if we move to the right ?

The Enterprise Continuum provides a .... to support the .... in executing the ADM. These ... may include A..., as explained in Part V: Enterprise Continuum & Tools : Note everything.

The practical implementation of the .... will typically take the form of an ... that .... enterprise. The architect would ... at hand. (In addition to the .....).

Answer : A

Q 1123 Which of the following best describes the class of information known as the Architecture Capability within the Architecture Repository ?

A. A description of the organization specific architecture framework and method

B. A record of the governance activity across the enterprise

C. Guidelines and templates used to create new architectures

D. Processes to support governance of the Architecture Repository

Explanation :

Architecture Capability section within the Architecture Repository stores details about the very processes to support its own governance. Governance does not just mean the tasks of the Architecture Governance Board. It also covers all the directions given within EA department, by the superiors to others, in order that the tasks, progress and outputs are as per (tailored) TOGAF® framework and as per more fined-tuned guidelines supplied as best practices.

See under : **7.1 Overview**[56]

Operating a ... within .. creates ...

Effective management and leverage of these ... require .. for .. alongside .. and ....

This Architecture Repository is .., which provides ....

▪ The **Architecture Capability** defines the ....

Answer Choice A) A description of the organization specific architecture framework and method is about ADM and its metamodel as stored in the Architecture Repository.

---

55. https://pubs.opengroup.org/togaf-standard/adm/chap01.html#tag_01_01_01

56. https://pubs.opengroup.org/togaf-standard/architecture-content/chap07.html#tag_07_01

Answer Choice B) A record of the governance activity across the enterprise : is stored by the Governance Repository portion of the Architecture Repository. This portion stores the results of Compliance assessments etc.,

Answer Choice C) Guidelines and templates used to create new architectures : is about the Reference Library portion of the Architecture Repository.

Answer : D

NON-CONVENTIONAL MULTIPLE choice questions start from here. Go through them with attention since such questions are hallmark of TOGAF® 10 Exam

Q 1150

Refer to the image below

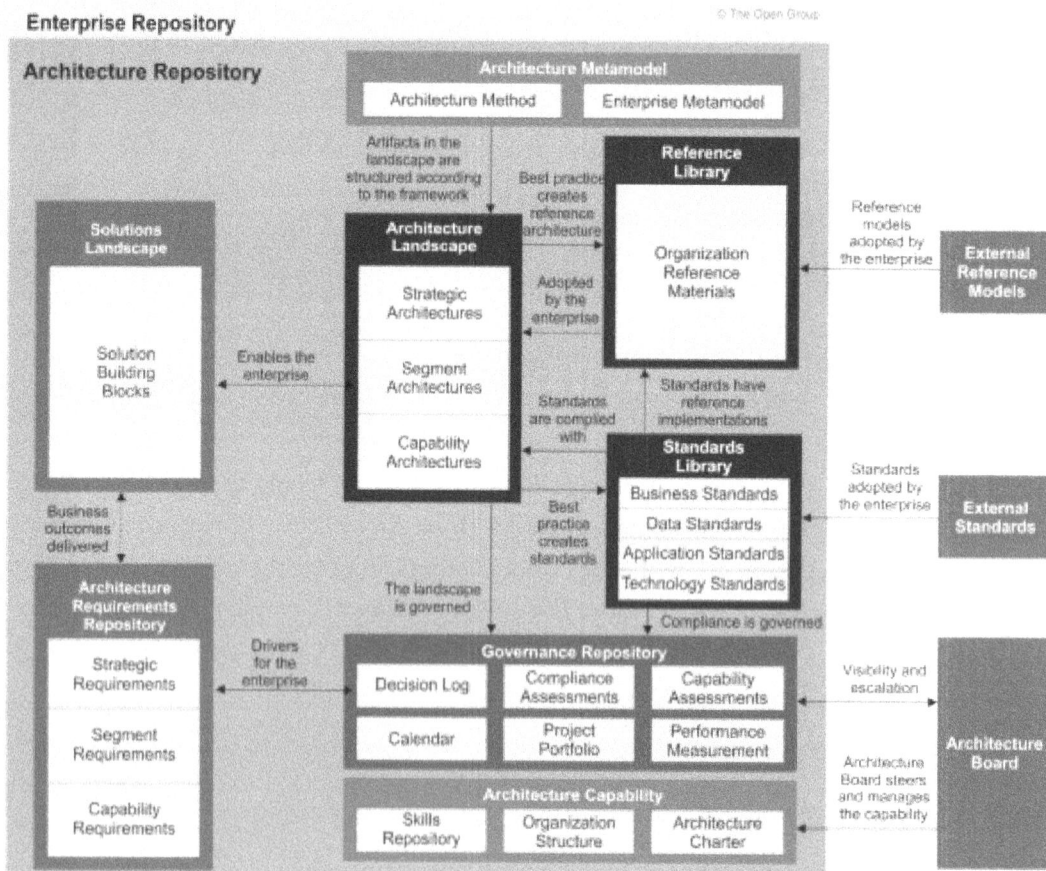

PICK THE CORRECT COMBINATION of True / False with respect to statements in the Table below, while referring to the image above

1 Governance Repository defines the parameters, structures, and processes that support governance of the Architecture Repository

2 The Architecture Requirements Repository provides a view of all authorized architecture requirements which have been agreed with the Architecture Board

3 The Solutions Landscape presents an architectural representation of the SBBs supporting the Architecture Landscape which have been planned or deployed by the enterprise

4 The image shows, at a high level, the classes of architectural information are expected to be held within an Architecture Repository

A. 1 – True 2 – True 3 – True 4 – True

B. 1 – False 2 – True 3 – False 4 –True

C. 1 – False 2 – True 3 – True 4 – True

D. 1 – True 2 – True 3 – True 4 – False

Explanation :

Refer to : **7.1 Overview**[57]

Read the two statements therein :

The Governance Repository provides a record of governance activity across the Enterprise

The Architecture Capability defines the parameters, structures, and processes that support governance of the Architecture Repository

Answer : C

57. https://pubs.opengroup.org/togaf-standard/architecture-content/chap07.html#tag_07_01

Q 1151

Refer to the image below :

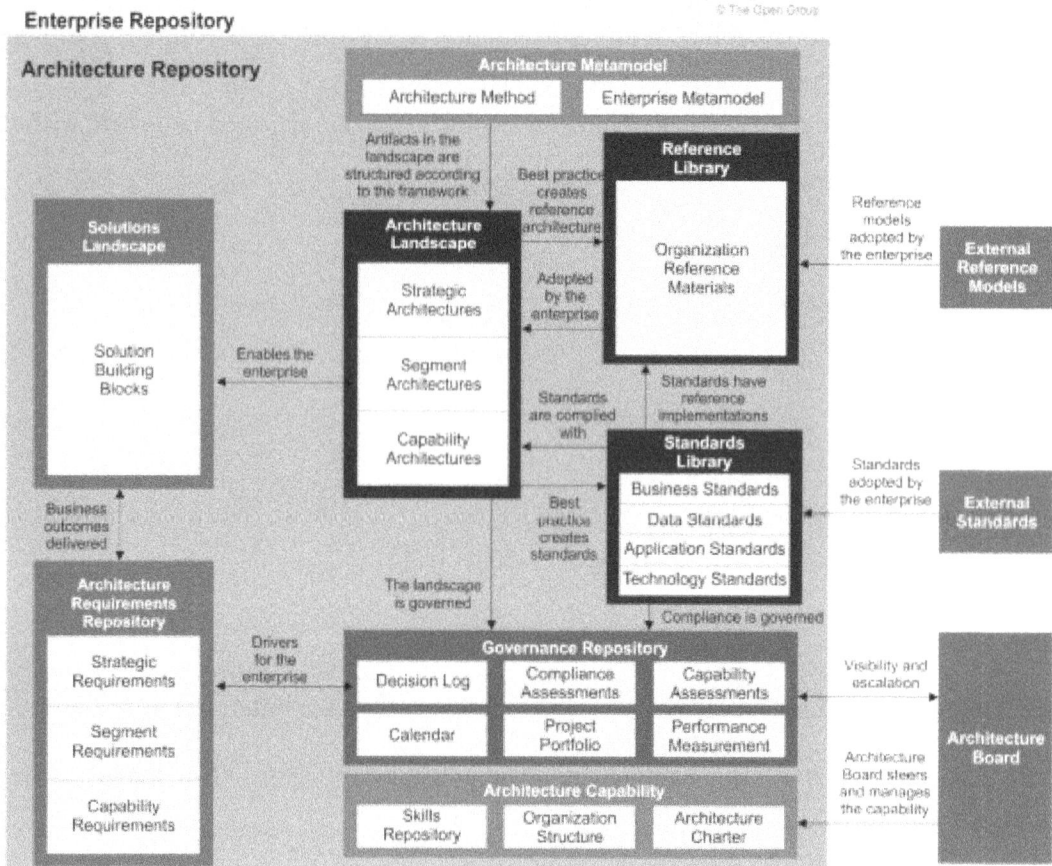

SPOT THE INCORRECT statement, which is regarding one particular section of the image

A. Decision Log : a log of all architecturally significant decisions that have been made in the organization
B. Compliance Assessments are carried out only towards the end of a project, and is meant to measure the progress
C. Performance Measurement is based on a charter for the architecture function, a number of performance criteria will typically be defined
D. Capability Assessments : depending on their objectives, some projects will carry out assessments of business, IT, or Architecture Capability. These assessments should be periodically carried out and tracked to ensure that appropriate progress is being made

Explanation :

See : **7.5.2 Contents of the Governance Repository**[58] :

Note the statement : Compliance Assessments : at ... in the ...of a project, a formal ... will be carried out. This .. will measure the ... to the ... standards

---

58. https://pubs.opengroup.org/togaf-standard/architecture-content/chap07.html#tag_07_05_02

It need not be conducted towards the end of implementation only. Intermediate and periodical ones can also be planned.

Answer : B

Module 12 : Content Framework
and Enterprise Metamodel

———

References shown as 'See' herein refer to :

2. TOGAF® Content Framework and Enterprise Metamodel[1] under Architecture Content part of TOGAF® Standard Fundamental Content Version 10

In case any other free-standing document of TOGAF® Standard Fundamental Content Version 10 or Series Guide is referenced, that is explicitly mentioned.

Q 1201 There are a number of architectural work products or artifacts, such as process and application. What defines a formal structure for these terms to ensure consistency within the ADM ?

A. Enterprise Metamodel

B. Content Framework

C. Architecture Landscape

D. Content Framework and Enterprise Metamodel

Explanation :

See : **2.1 Overview**[2]

The Content Framework and Enterprise Metamodel define ... for these terms to ensure ... and also to ...

On the other hand,

The Architecture Landscape presents ....

It houses the ... and does not provide ...

Answer : D

———

Q 1202 Which part of TOGAF® Standard Fundamental Content Version 10 defines a categorization framework to be used to structure the Architecture ?

A. ADM Techniques portion of TOGAF® Standard Fundamental Content Version 10

B. Enterprise Architecture Capability and Governance part of TOGAF® Standard Fundamental Content Version 10

C. Architecture Development Method part of TOGAF® Standard Fundamental Content Version 10

---

1. https://pubs.opengroup.org/togaf-standard/architecture-content/chap02.html#tag_02

2. https://pubs.opengroup.org/togaf-standard/architecture-content/chap02.html#tag_02_01

D. Architecture Content part of TOGAF® Standard Fundamental Content Version 10

Explanation :

See : **1.2.2 Content Framework**[3] : Architecture Content part of TOGAF® Standard Fundamental Content Version 10 :

The ... defines a ... framework to be used to ...

Answer Choice A) ADM Techniques portion of TOGAF® Standard Fundamental Content Version 10 : not categorization, but (**architectural**) **process guidelines.**

Answer Choice B) Enterprise Architecture Capability and Governance part of TOGAF® Standard Fundamental Content Version 10 : not categorization, but **a sub-Framework** within TOGAF®.

Answer Choice C) Architecture Development Method part of TOGAF® Standard Fundamental Content Version 10 : not categorization, but (**architectural**) **process description, phase by phase.**

Also See : **2.1 Overview**[4]

The Content Framework defines a ... framework to be used to ..., the ... used to express an ..., and the .. that describe the architecture.

Answer : D

Q 1203 The selection of Content Framework is not influenced by certain criterion. Pick the wrong statement

A. As a basis for Enterprise Architecture Capability

B. The specific software Tool selected to produce the Architecture content

C. Tool selection, since any tool can produce the content

D. None of the above

Explanation :

See : **1.2.1 Overview**[5]

The Content Framework chosen is ... by :

- The ... selected as the basis for the ...
- The ... used to ...

Answer : C

---

3. https://pubs.opengroup.org/togaf-standard/architecture-content/chap01.html#tag_01_02_02

4. https://pubs.opengroup.org/togaf-standard/architecture-content/chap02.html#tag_02_01

5. https://pubs.opengroup.org/togaf-standard/architecture-content/chap01.html#tag_01_02_01

Q 1204 Pick the incorrect statement about TOGAF® enterprise Metamodel

A. Not meant to capture Entities and relationships therein

B. Can lead to Organization Specific Metamodel

C. Useful in establishing the Enterprise Architecture Capability in Preliminary Phase onwards

D. Provides the context for the specific artifacts referenced in the descriptions of the ADM phase

Explanation :

See : **2.2 TOGAF® Enterprise Metamodel Vision**[6]

TOGAF® Enterprise Metamodel ....

This may be used as the ... and also ....

Answer : A

Q 1205 Which of the TOGAF® Components describe the organizationally tailored application of an architecture framework, including a metamodel for architecture content

A. Architecture Capability

B. Architecture Landscape

C. Architecture Metamodel

D. Reference Library

E. Governance Repository

Explanation :

See : **3.11 Architecture Repository**[7] : under Introduction and Core Concepts part of TOGAF® Standard Fundamental Content Version 10

The ..... describes the ... of an architecture framework, including ...

It is nice to get to know the following portions also, to be prepared for few other questions :

Supporting the ... which can be used to .., created by the ADM.

In this way, the TOGAF® Standard facilitates ,,,.

By means of the ..., architects are ....

In this context, the ...regarded as ..., operating within ... and producing ...

6. https://pubs.opengroup.org/togaf-standard/architecture-content/chap02.html#tag_02_02

7. https://pubs.opengroup.org/togaf-standard/introduction/chap03.html#tag_03_11

The .... provides a ... for understanding ..: it shows .., and the ...

Answer : C

NON-CONVENTIONAL MULTIPLE choice questions start from here. Go through them with attention since such questions are hallmark of TOGAF® 10 Exam

Q 1250

Consider the following statements, look into them being true or false and then set to pick the right combination :

1 The TOGAF® ADM does not provide a lifecycle management system to create and manage architectures within an enterprise. At each phase within the ADM, a discussion of inputs, outputs, and steps describes a number of architectural work products

An essential task when establishing the enterprise-specific Enterprise Architecture Capability in the Preliminary Phase of the ADM is to define:

2
- A categorization framework to be used to structure the Architecture Descriptions, the work products used to express an architecture, and the collection of models that describe the architecture; this is referred to as the Content Framework

An essential task when establishing the enterprise-specific Enterprise Architecture Capability in the Preliminary Phase of the ADM is to also to define :

3
- An understanding of the types of entities within the enterprise and the relationships between them that need to be captured, stored, and analysed in order to create the Architecture Description; this Enterprise Metamodel depicts this information in the form of a formal model
- The specific artifacts to be developed

The Content Framework chosen is likely to be influenced by:

4
- The Architecture Framework selected as the basis for the Enterprise Architecture Capability
- The chosen software tool used to support the Enterprise Architecture Capability

Which of the following is correct ?

A. 1 False – 2 False – 3 False – 4 False

B. 1 False – 2 False – 3 False – 4 True

C. 1 False – 2 True – 3. False - 4 True

D. 1 False – 2 True – 3 True – 4 True

Explanation :

See **3.12 TOGAF® Content Framework and Enterprise Metamodel**[8] : under Introduction and Core Concepts part of TOGAF® Standard Fundamental Content Version 10

Row 1) should have read as :

The TOGAF® ADM provides ... to create and manage ... enterprise.

At each phase within the ADM, ... of ...describes a ... products

Answer : D

Q 1251

Refer to the image below :

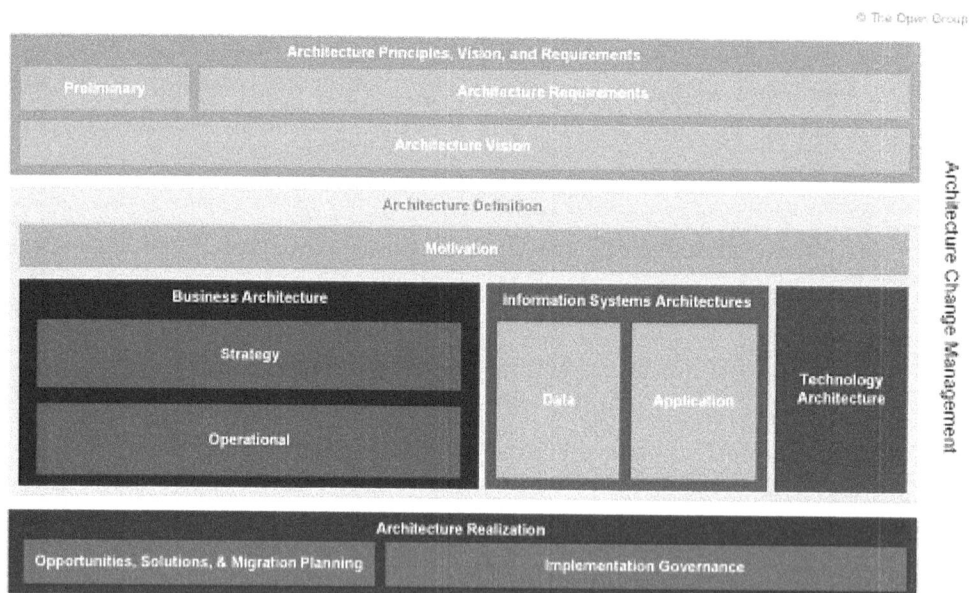

SPOT THE INCORRECT statement among the following :

A. The Content Framework defines a categorization framework to be used to describe the building blocks and artifacts reflecting decisions taken in creating the overall architecture deliverables. So, it is same as the Architecture Repository.
B. There are many alternative Content Frameworks (e.g., the TOGAF® Content Framework, the Zachman Framework, DoDAF, NAF, etc.).
C. Selecting a Content Framework is essential even though the choice of Content Framework is less important.
D. The final Content Framework is usually adapted to fit specific organization needs.

Explanation :

See : **3.12.2 Content Framework**[9] : under Introduction and Core Concepts part of TOGAF® Standard Fundamental Content Version 10

The Content Framework ... a **categorization framework** to be used ...

So, it cannot be the same as the Architecture Repository.

The Architecture Repository is .. **to store** the ...... identified in the Content Framework.

The Content Framework is ... Architecture Framework

Also read about : The TOGAF® Content Framework is intended to:

- Provide a ... Drive consistency ... Provide a ...
- Reduce the ... Help an ... and deliverables

Answer : A

———————————

IT IS NICE TO READ the following and be prepared for questions that could surprise us :

See **8.3 What Constitutes the Content Metamodel ?** [10] : under TOGAF® Series Guide : The TOGAF® Leader's Guide to Establishing and Evolving an EA Capability

Regarding information management, the ... must have at hand.

In practical terms, ... and the information that ....

Consider what .. two questions :

- How can the ... ?
- What ... its product ?

The Content Metamodel is ... portfolio ?".

The difficulty comes when, .. to answer :

◈ Which processes ... ?

◈ Which processes ... ?

◈ What ... ?

◈ What is ... ?

There are two approaches to ... the focus.

In this case, ... in future.

---

9. https://pubs.opengroup.org/togaf-standard/introduction/chap03.html#tag_03_12_02

10. https://pubs.opengroup.org/togaf-standard/togaf-leaders-guide/togaf-leaders-guide_8.html#_Toc95220389

Following this approach ...consistently failed.

An alternative practice is to ... requires.

In either case, ... of each other.

Every component that is ... stated purpose.

Recommendation from ... the viewpoint library.

Explore the ... and nothing more.

Consider what ... more aspects of the enterprise.

The exercise is not to .. asked of the EA Capability.

The TOGAF® Content Metamodel ... with the EA Capability's purpose.

To answer these stakeholder questions, ... with appropriate intersections.

It is rare, but possible, to have ... pre-packaged metamodels.

Module 13 : Enterprise Continuum

Note that questions do come up with answer choices and correct answer picked up from other modules beyond these. Revisit all questions after revising the whole of TOGAF®.

Cross References shown as 'See' herein refer to : **6. Enterprise Continuum**[1] under Architecture Content part of TOGAF® Standard Fundamental Content Version 10

In case any other free-standing document of TOGAF® Standard Fundamental Content Version 10 or Series Guide is referenced, that is explicitly mentioned.

Q 1301 Which of the following architectures in the Architecture Continuum contains the most re-usable architecture elements ?

A. Common Systems Architectures

B. Foundation Architectures

C. Industry Architectures

D. Organization-Specific Architectures

Explanation :

It is obvious that Foundation Architectures, lying in top-left corner of Enterprise Continuum will have maximum re-use potential. It will not only be used in building rest of three Architectures in Architecture Continuum but also in the Solutions Continuum.

See under : **6.4.1 Architecture Continuum : Foundation Architecture**[2]

A Foundation Architecture consists of ... that provide a .... : What all does it consisting of ? What does it support ?

The TOGAF® ADM is a process ... specialization of such ... in order to create ..

The ... is an example of a Foundation Architecture. It is a ... upon which ... can be based.

See under : **6.3 Constituents of the Enterprise Continuum**[3]

The Architecture Continuum offers ... in an architecture, including ... to show that ... is based on an ...: Study why this is about the evolution or the progression of the architectural assets.

The Architecture Continuum represents ... which are ... assets.

ABBs evolve through ...from ... to ....

---

1. **https://pubs.opengroup.org/togaf-standard/architecture-content/chap06.html**

2. **https://pubs.opengroup.org/togaf-standard/architecture-content/chap06.html#tag_06_04_01_01**

3. **https://pubs.opengroup.org/togaf-standard/architecture-content/chap06.html#tag_06_03**

Re-Use, Re-Use, Re-Use : The focus of TOGAF® on Re-Use of Architectural assets.

Answer : B

———————

Q 1302 Which of the following best describes TOGAF® Technical Reference Model ?

A. It is a detailed data model that can be tailored to specific industries

B. It is an example of a Common Systems Architecture

C. It is a fundamental architecture upon which more specific architectures can be based

D. It is a model of application components and application services software, including brokering applications

Explanation :

The very reason why TRM is placed under Foundation Architecture is based on the fact that by itself the Architecture therein is fundamental and the Actual project Architecture must be built upon it.

For Answer Choice A) Detailed data models are not part of TRM. Note that it is a "technical" reference model.

For Answer Choice B) III-RM is cited as an example of Common Systems Architecture.

For Answer Choice D) It refers to a model that is developed more on the lines of III-RM.

See under : **6.4.1 : Foundation Architecture**[4]

A Foundation Architecture consists of ... that provide a .. on which more .. can be built.

The TOGAF® ADM is a ... in order to ..

The .. is an example of ...

It is a .. upon which other, ... can be based.

Answer : C

For knowledge beyond Exam syllabus on this, refer to : TOGAF® Series Guide: The TOGAF® Technical Reference Model (TRM)[5]

———————

Q 1303 Which of the following best describes the III-RM

A. It is a detailed data model that can be tailored to specific industries

B. It is an example of a Common Systems Architecture

C. It is a fundamental architecture upon which more specific architectures can be based

———————

4. https://pubs.opengroup.org/togaf-standard/architecture-content/chap06.html#tag_06_04_01_01

5. https://pubs.opengroup.org/togaf-standard/reference-models/trm.html

D. It is a model of application components and application services software, including brokering applications

Explanation :

III-RM deals with elements on Service Provider and Service Consumer and so it is a grouping of basic elements, qualifying itself to be a Common Systems Architecture.

On wrong Answer Choices :

Answer Choice A) : It is a detailed data model that can be tailored to specific industries – III-RM is a Communication Model among applications and not at all a Data Model.

Answer Choice C) : It is a fundamental architecture upon which more specific architectures can be based – This definition applies to more fundamental elements like those in TRM. However, III-RM is built over the Foundation Architecture to suggest a collaborative architecture.

Answer Choice D) : It is a model of application components and application services software, including brokering applications – Point is true, but it is not the best description of III-RM. See under : **6.4.1 : Common Systems Architectures**[6]

The TOGAF® Integrated Information Infrastructure Reference Model (III-RM) — is a .. that supports describing ... in the .. Domain that focuses on the ...: Focusses on what ? Relates to what ?

Answer : B

For knowledge beyond Exam syllabus on this, refer to : TOGAF® Series Guide : <u>The TOGAF® Integrated Information Infrastructure Reference Model (III-RM)</u>[7]

Q 1304 Which of the following architectures in the Architecture Continuum would possibly contain the least re-usable architecture elements ?

A. Common Systems Architectures

B. Organization-Specific Architectures

C. Foundation Architectures

D. Industry Architectures

Explanation :

It is obvious that Organization-Specific Architectures, lying in top-right corner of Architecture Continuum will have minimum re-use potential while formulating ABBs. It will not be shared with other competing organizations. It can only be referred to internally in future projects, if a reason for re-use is justified.

See : **<u>6.4.1 Architecture Continuum : Organization-Specific Architectures</u>**[8]

Organization-Specific Architectures describe ... the final ... for a ...

---

6. https://pubs.opengroup.org/togaf-standard/architecture-content/chap06.html#tag_06_04_01_02

7. https://pubs.opengroup.org/togaf-standard/reference-models/iiirm.html

8. https://pubs.opengroup.org/togaf-standard/architecture-content/chap06.html#tag_06_04_01_04

There may be a ... that are needed to ... by defining the .... : What do they define ? How does it differ in case of global enterprises ?

Alternatively, this might result in .... for ...

The Organization-Specific Architecture guides the ..., and has the following characteristics : (Guides what ?)

▪ Provides a means to .... and ... business ... across all four ... : A way to manage business related operations over D, A, T segments. Also for effective communication on the same.

▪ Reflects .... specific to a ... : A reflation of the requirements, but in the form of ABBs. TOGAF® uses the term 'Requirement' to mean Stakeholder based concerns which are captured as just stated Requirements as also for all ABB work carried out thereon.

▪ Defines ... specific to a ... : Though based on Foundational and Common System Blocks, or drawn from Industry Specific Blocks, they become highly specific to your Enterprise when it reaches this stage.

▪ Contains organization-specific ...,...., ..., and .... : See what models it talks about here.

▪ Provides a means to ... of ... to meet business needs : Solutions that would subsequently emanate, but from what needs ? Very important point.

▪ Provides the criteria to .... and ... appropriate ..., ..., and ...s : Serves as a basis for selections as mentioned here and even as the benchmark against the selected ones as a measure.

▪ Provides an .... to support ... and .. needs : Business needs and business capability grows based on each set of Organizational Specific Architectural output, each being a re-use basis for a future one. New needs of business and capability is also built likewise.

Answer : B

———————

Q 1305 Which one of the following represents the detailed construction of the architectures defined in the Architecture Continuum ?

A. Architecture Building Blocks

B. Conceptual Models

C. Foundation Architectures

D. Reference Models

E. Solution Building Blocks

Explanation :

The Solutions Continuum defines what is available in the organizational environment as re-usable Solution Building Blocks (SBBs).

See : **6.3 Constituents of the Enterprise Continuum**[9]

The **Architecture Continuum**[10] offers ..., including .. (e.g., to show ..). : Define and understand what ? What is the relationship mentioned here ? Each one here is important.

The Architecture Continuum represents a structuring of ... Blocks (..) which are ... assets. ABBs evolve ... from .. and ... to fully expressed ...assets. The Architecture Continuum assets will be used to ... the elements in the ...Continuum : Note phrases like 'structuring of' , 'reusable' 'assets' 'development lifecycle' and so on.

The Architecture Continuum shows the ..... foundational ...(such as ...), ... architectures (such as ....), ...architectures, and ... architectures. The Architecture Continuum is a useful tool to ..... and ... redundancy : What is the relationship cited here ? What is mentioned as an 'useful tool' for what ?

The **Solutions Continuum**[11] provides a ...way to ... and ...the .... of the ...defined in the ... Continuum. The ...Continuum defines .....as re-usable .. Blocks (...). The solutions are the ...of ... between ... and ... that ... the rules and ... defined in the .. space. The.... Continuum addresses the ...and ... among the ..., systems, and ...of ...systems : Which Continuum is there for 'understanding and implementation' of what is mentioned in the above two paragraphs ? What does it define ? What does it address ? Where does the results transform to ? (Relate this paragraph to Architecture Contracts mentioned in Phase G)

Answer : A

Q 1306 An association of companies in the same line of business has defined a data model for sharing inventory and pricing information. Which of the following best describes where this model would fit in the Architecture Continuum ?

A. Foundation Architecture

B. Common Systems Architecture

C. Industry Architecture

D. Organization Specific Architecture

E. Product Line Architecture

Explanation :

This association is an industry association. They have produced Reference Architecture for this industry.

See : **6.4.1 Architecture Continuum : Industry Architectures**[12]

Industry Architectures guide the integration of .... with .... components and guide the ... of industry .... for targeted .... within a particular industry : Integration of what with what ?

9. https://pubs.opengroup.org/togaf-standard/architecture-content/chap06.html#tag_06_03

10. https://pubs.opengroup.org/togaf-standard/architecture-content/chap06.html#tag_06_04_01

11. https://pubs.opengroup.org/togaf-standard/architecture-content/chap06.html#tag_06_04_02

12. https://pubs.opengroup.org/togaf-standard/architecture-content/chap06.html#tag_06_04_01_04

A typical example of an ...., or an Industry Architecture that incorporates the .... : Make it a point to remember various such branded industry specific Architecture. It is Active Store and Energetics here. ARTS and TMF elsewhere. Which industry does each one pertains to ? Also figure out if it is a data model technology model or what else!

Other characteristics of Industry Architectures include :

▪ Reflects ....and ....specific to a ... industry : Both requirements (see what is mentioned in explanation of **Q 1304** about the way TOGAF® treats the term 'Requirement') and standards are to be specific to a vertical. Not Foundational or Common Systems ones that will appear here.

▪ Defines .... specific to a ... domain : Building Blocks and artifacts in them are specific.

▪ Contains industry-specific .. and ... : All models and logic therein are also specific.

▪ Contains industry-specific ... and process models, as well as industry-specific business rules : Not just application and their logical models, but rules embedded in them are also specific.

▪ Provides .... for .... collections of ...: Includes such guidelines.

▪ Encourages levels of .... throughout the ...: Promotes and prompts the concept of interoperability of Components and Services between Enterprises operating in the same vertical industry.

Answer : C

Q 1307 Where does the Integrated Information Infrastructure Reference Model fit in terms of the Enterprise Continuum ?

A. Common Systems Architectures

B. Foundation Architectures

C. Industry Architectures

D. Organization-Specific Architectures

Explanation :

See : **6.3 Constituents of the Enterprise Continuum**[13]

The Architecture Continuum shows ... (such as the ...), ... (such as the ...), ..., and ...

The TOGAF® Integrated Information Infrastructure Reference Model (III-RM) is a Common Systems Architecture that focuses on the requirements, building blocks, and standards relating to the vision of Boundaryless Information Flow™.

Refer to TOGAF® Series Guide on "III-RM" : **(III-RM)SeriesGuide**[14] : **1.1 Background**[15]

---

13. https://pubs.opengroup.org/togaf-standard/architecture-content/chap06.html#tag_06_03

14. https://pubs.opengroup.org/togaf-standard/reference-models/iiirm.html

15. https://pubs.opengroup.org/togaf-standard/reference-models/iiirm.html#_Toc513188167

With the ..... in recent years, for many organizations the main ...., and the ... in architecture effort, has shifted from the ... to the .... (Indeed, this has been .... behind the migration of TOGAF® itself from .. for ... to one for ... architecture).

The TOGAF® ... Model, ..., focuses on the ... space.

This .... a reference model that focuses on the .... space, and "....." in Enterprise Continuum terms. This is the ....Model (...) : Focus on what space ?

The ...is a subset of the .... in terms of its ...., but it also .... - in particular, the .. and ... parts - in order to provide help in addressing ... .architect today: the need to .... to enable ... Flow : Understand the relationship between the two.

Answer : A

Q 1308 In the views of Enterprise Continuum, evolution is not seen as

A. Abstract to Concrete

B. Generic to specific

C. Strategic to Segment

D. Logical to Physical

Explanation :

Strategic, Segment and Capability are levels of partitioning of the Architecture. They evolve over the years to produce projects.

But the question is about evolution of Enterprise Continuum, which means the way an Architect look at it to get increasing focussed content for use of the projects.

See : **1.4 The Enterprise Continuum**[16] : 1. Introduction under Architecture Content part of TOGAF® Standard Fundamental Content Version 10

It is usually .... to create a single .... that meets all ... of all ... for all .... Therefore, the Enterprise Architect will need to deal ....., but with many .... Architectures : The need is to deal with (what all ?)

Each ... will have a .... and ...will relate to one another : What could be different from each to others ?

Effectively ..... is therefore a .. (...) in allowing architects to ... a complex ... into manageable ... that can be ... : What is the critical factor here ? What is to be addressed individually ?

The Enterprise ....provides a view of the ... that shows the .... from ... to ..., from ... to ... and from ... to ...: Important point. Of the answer choices here, two are the same and is seen in the corresponding diagram as top row to bottom row. What are they ?

Also see : **3.2 Architecture Landscape**[17]

---

16. https://pubs.opengroup.org/togaf-standard/architecture-content/chap01.html#tag_01_04

17. https://pubs.opengroup.org/togaf-standard/applying-the-adm/chap03.html#tag_03_02

1. **Strategic Architecture** provides ...

2. **Segment Architecture** provides ...

Answer : C

Q 1309 Solutions Continuum is all the following except

A. Non-Architecture solutions

B. A consistent way to describe and understand the implementation of the Architecture Continuum

C. A consistent way to look at the implementation of the ABBs

D. A progression so solutions from generic level to specific level

Explanation :

When we talk about Enterprise Continuum and Solutions Continuum, we mean only an index to Architectural Content.

Anything that is not architectural in nature but is about a solution may have to be stored elsewhere and viewed through another mechanism. Say a negotiation strategy for sales is not an architectural content.

SEE UNDER : **6.3 Constituents of the Enterprise Continuum**[18]

The **Solutions Continuum** provides a .... to describe and ...the ... of the .... in the Architecture ... : Which describes in a consistent way and what ?

The Solutions Continuum defines .... environment as ... Blocks (...). The ... are the results of ... that .... defined in the ... space. The ... Continuum addresses the ... and ...mong the ... systems : Get to know each of the point here.

Also see : **6.4.2 Solutions Continuum**[19]

The Solutions Continuum represents the ... and .. of the architectures at the .... of the .. Continuum : Represents what ? It is about the specification of the solution, duly expressed as architectural artifacts (such as Catalog, Matrix and more than these two through appropriate diagrams along with accompanying descriptions. Since these are SBBs, construction details, meaning assembly of each block will be part of these. Can even be the development platform details and more information and idioms thereon. It is also said that each may be a concrete and physical translation of corresponding ABBs in the Architecture Continuum.

At each level, the Solutions Continuum is a population of the ...with ... blocks — either .... or built ...— that represent a ... to the enterprise's ... expressed at that level : These SBBs may be referencing other blocks and could be branded and purchased products (can be hardware, software or even subscriptions and licences to Software As a Service and other offerings) or they could be custom built by your Enterprise. In effect they will be representative of the solution

---

18. https://pubs.opengroup.org/togaf-standard/architecture-content/chap06.html#tag_06_03

19. https://pubs.opengroup.org/togaf-standard/architecture-content/chap06.html#tag_06_04_02

(meaning they are not yet implemented – coded or installed - but are architectures that are so detailed that they can be implemented easily from these), but are based on a business need expressed by the respective Stakeholders.

A ... based on the .... Continuum can be regarded as a ... or ... library, which can add .... to the task of ... improvements to the enterprise : See how these are pointed to as an inventory of solutions (artifacts) and have high re-use potential. What will be the value added by them ?

Answer : A

Q 1310 Foundation Solutions is about all the following except

A. Highly generic Solution concepts, that are ready for implementation

B. Can comprise of Tools, Products and Services

C. Provider of Capability, buy still stay at a fundamental level

D. Not a Capability builder because it is too generic

EXPLANATION :

A Foundation Solution is just a artifact or stand-alone component that forms a SBB. It is difficult to state exactly which Capability for the Enterprise can be built with it. Being a foundation solution, it will find its use in many capabilities.

For example the architecture that explains how a socket is to be implemented under a specific technology platform will find its use in almost every Capability (Transition) Architecture that involves networking.

See under : **6.4.2 : Foundation Solutions**[20]

Foundation Solutions ...., ..., ..., ..., and ... components that are the .. providers of .... Services include ... — such ... services — that ensure the ... time; and ...services — such as ... — that ensure the ...from solutions (services that ensure ... to the products and systems) : So generic that they point to single capability, among the list mentioned here of 'generic concepts, tools, products, services'. Get a good grasp of services mentioned here and what is following the 'ensure' phrase in each of them.

Example Foundation Solutions would .... operations (such as ....or the ... Architecture) etc., : Make a note of the examples cited here.

Answer : D

Q 1311 Common System Solution is about all the following except

A. An implementation of a Common Systems Architecture

B. Can comprise of industry specific Architectures that is common only to a few industries

C. Collections of common requirements and capabilities

D. Can be branded or certified

Explanation :

Take a Security solution for Authentication and Authorization, using a specific cryptography and specific mechanism for log-in situations in Dot Net projects :

An implementation of a Common Systems Architecture – Based on a platform independent architecture for Authentication and Authorization.

Collections of common requirements and capabilities – This is a very common ned in user centric projects; Capability is : authentication is the process of verifying oneself, while authorization is the process of verifying what resources that person have access to. Can be branded or certified – already branded for use such as "only under Dot Net Web projects".

See under : **6.4.2 : Common Systems Solutions**[21]

A Common Systems Solution is an .... of a ... Architecture comprised of a ...., which may be .... It represents .... for one or more solutions in the ... that the Common Systems Solution supports : Always a group. Component as set. Branded means it is of a named technology, just like the Dot Net in the example above. The term 'Certified' is used to indicate how a vendor may brand it and attached to a named item. What is the 'highest common denominator' that is mentioned here ?

Common .... represent collections of ... and ... rather than those specific to a ..... Common .... provide organizations with ... specific to ... and ...needs, such as .... and ... systems : What is the collection mentioned ? What is the environment mentioned ? (Hint : Operations is more aligned to application and infrastructure while informational is more aligned to data systems). Study the two 'needs' that are taken for the example here.

Examples of Common Systems Solutions include: ... product. Computer systems ... technology-centric ... Solutions. "Software as a service" vendors are typical ... solutions. Business process outsourcing vendors are ... Common Systems Solutions : Do understand the examples given.

Answer : B

———————

Q 1312 This one is not specific to an Industry

A. Solution templates and guidelines for Banking industry

B. Solution templates and guidelines for Healthcare industry

C. Solution templates and guidelines for Merchandising industry

D. Solution templates and guidelines for your Enterprise

Explanation :

---

21. https://pubs.opengroup.org/togaf-standard/architecture-content/chap06.html#tag_06_04_02_02

What is specific to an "industry" (like Banking industry) cannot also be specific to an "Enterprise" (such as Central Bank of ...).

Also read from : **6.4.2 : Industry Solutions**[22]

An Industry Solution is an .... of an Industry Architecture, which provides ... of common ... specific to an industry : What does it provide 'specifically' ? What is suggested as 're-usable' here ?

Fundamental components are provided by .... Solutions and/or ... Solutions and are augmented with ... components. Examples include: ... device : How is this related to Foundation Solutions ?

Industry Solutions are industry-specific.... that are ready to ... requirements. In some cases an .... may include not only an ... Architecture, but also ... such as ...., ..., and ... that are appropriate to that industry : What do they aggregate ? What more is to be tailored ? Is this same as Tailoring TOGAF® seen in Preliminary Phase ? (Hint : In Preliminary Phase we tailor the framework. Here the mention is about tailoring a portion of the solution. Both are poles apart). What are the 'other solution elements' mentioned here ?

Answer : D

Q 1313 Complete the sentence. As the architecture evolves, the assets in the Solutions Continuum progress towards a(n) _____

A. Common Systems Architecture

B. Industry Specific Architecture

C. Foundation Solution

D. Organization Specific Solution

E. Technology Neutral Implementation

Explanation :

The very idea of having a Solution Continuum is to start with basic contents which evolve till they become content to be used by our Enterprise and its departments (Organization Specific Solution).

See : **6.4.2 Solutions Continuum**[23]

The Solutions Continuum represents ... at the ...of the Architecture Continuum.

At each level, the Solutions Continuum is ... — either ... or ... — that represent ....

A ... based on the Solutions Continuum can be ... or ..., which can ... to the task of ....

---

22. https://pubs.opengroup.org/togaf-standard/architecture-content/chap06.html#tag_06_04_02_03

23. https://pubs.opengroup.org/togaf-standard/architecture-content/chap06.html#tag_06_04_02

"Moving to the right" on the .... Continuum is focused on ... value (i.e., ... provide value in ...; .... solutions are used to create ... solutions; and ...solutions are used to create .. solutions) : What is the value mentioned here as successive ones ? Study all 'moving to' that appears under the topic of Enterprise Continuum.

"Moving to the left" on the Solutions Continuum is focused on addressing enterprise (wide) needs.

Answer Choices A) and B) are about Architecture Continuum, while the question is about Solutions Continuum.

Answer Choices C) Foundation Solution is at the left-most of the blocks and cannot qualify for a destination of 'progress towards'.

Answer : D

Q 1314 Which pair of the following responses best completes the sentence : Architecture Building Blocks _____, whereas Solution Building Blocks _____

A. are assembled; are single function components

B. are single function components; are groups of architecture Building Blocks

C. are reusable; are not reusable

D. define the architecture; provide the existing legacy system

E. define functionality; define the implementation of functionality

Explanation :

Architecture Building Blocks define functionality whereas Solution Building Blocks ; define the implementation of functionality. This is the very definition of the two kind of Building Blocks.

Looking into : **5.2.3.1 Characteristics**[24] and **5.2.3.2 Specification Content**[25] : **Architecture Building Blocks** : 5. Building Blocks under Architecture Content part of TOGAF® Standard Fundamental Content Version 10

ABBs : ▪ Capture ....; e.g., ..., and ..y requirements

▪ ... and ... the development of ...

5.2.3.2 Specification Content[26] : ABB specifications include the following as a minimum :

▪ Fundamental ... : ... and .... ▪ Interfaces : ...set, ...

▪ ....and .... with other ... ▪ Dependent ... with ... and ..

▪ Map to ......

Do refer back to explanation appearing under **Q 608**

---

24. https://pubs.opengroup.org/togaf-standard/architecture-content/chap05.html#tag_05_02_03_01

25. https://pubs.opengroup.org/togaf-standard/architecture-content/chap05.html#tag_05_02_03_02

26. https://pubs.opengroup.org/togaf-standard/architecture-content/chap05.html#tag_05_02_03_02

5.2.4 Solution Building Blocks : 5.2.4.1 Characteristics[27] : SBBs :

- Define .. - Define ... - Fulfil ....

- Are.... or ... - aware

5.4.2 Specification Content[28] : SBB specifications include the following as a minimum :

- Specific ..... : Meaning, implementation of functionality

- Interfaces; the ... set : Definition of the exposed interfaces, such as API in Microservices, with implementation specific details of its parameters of functions and the like.

- Required SBBs used with ..... and ..... interfaces used : What does the service behind the interface meant for – revealed through named interface details.

- Mapping from the SBBs to the .... and ... : Connecting to hosting topology; What policies bind the operational specifics.

- Specifications of attributes .... environment (not to be confused with functionality) such as ... : Take good look at the NFRs (Non Functional Requirements) mentioned these being also known as Quality Attributes

- Performance, configurability : More NFR and the way they could be configured.

- Design ....., including the ... architecture : Physical LLD – Low Level Design

- Relationships between ... : How the two Continuums relate.

Answer : E

Q 1315 An organization has bought a large enterprise application. As a result, which of the following could be included in the organization's Solutions Continuum ?

A. A reference implementation of the Foundation Architecture

B. A reference implementation of the Technical Reference Model for the organization

C. Architecture Building Blocks for the organizations' Industry-Specific Architecture

D. Detailed pricing information about the purchased products

E. Product information and technical specification for purchased products

Explanation :

The Solutions Continuum is a population of the architecture with reference building blocks – could be either purchased products or ones as built components - these being ones that represent a solution to the enterprise's business need

---

27. https://pubs.opengroup.org/togaf-standard/architecture-content/chap05.html#tag_05_02_04_01

28. https://pubs.opengroup.org/togaf-standard/architecture-content/chap05.html#tag_05_02_04_02

expressed at the appropriate level. But pricing information is not an architecture artifact. Answer choices A), B) and C) are not about the newly bought enterprise (say ERP) application.

See : **6.4.2 Solutions Continuum**[29] : The Solutions Continuum is a ..of the ...with ... – either ... or ... - that represent ....

The **Solutions Continuum** provides a ...to describe and understand the ... in the ...

The Solutions Continuum defines ... as ...

The solutions are the ... between .. that .. defined in the ...

The Solutions Continuum ... and ... among ....

The Solutions Continuum represents the .... and ...of the architectures at .... levels of the Architecture Continuum. At each level, the Solutions Continuum is a .... of the architecture with ... blocks — either .... or built ... — that represent a .... to the enterprise's ... need expressed at that level. A populated ....based on the Solutions Continuum can be regarded as a .... or ... library, which can add .... to the task of ... and ... improvements to the enterprise : It is a detailed specification. It is highly construction-aware with adequate though process going into the way the ABBs can be taken to LLD – Low Level Design and beyond.

Answer : E

Q 1316 According to TOGAF®, how is the Enterprise Continuum used in organizing and developing an architecture ?

A. To aid communication and understanding between architects

B. To coordinate with the other management frameworks in use

C. To describe how an architecture addresses stakeholder concerns

D. To evaluate how best to develop and implement an architecture

E. To help identify and understand business requirements

Explanation :

Enterprise Continuum is used in organizing and developing an architecture for improved communication and understanding between architects.

See : **6.1 Overview**[30] :

The Enterprise Continuum provides methods for classifying ... and ... artifacts, both .... and ... to the Architecture Repository, as they evolve from .... to ... : It is an indexed classification mechanism (for accessing) both ABB based architecture assets and SBB based solution artifacts.. Point to note is about the 'evolution' path mentioned here, and you can note that it goes from left to right in the images shown.

The Enterprise Continuum .. of ... has been designed with the ....

---

29. https://pubs.opengroup.org/togaf-standard/architecture-content/chap06.html#tag_06_04_02

30. https://pubs.opengroup.org/togaf-standard/architecture-content/chap06.html#tag_06_01

The Enterprise Continuum is an ...aid to ... and ... both within .., and ...

Answer Choice B) To coordinate with the other management frameworks in use : Done as part of ADM, especially in Phase F. Enterprise Continuum is only about architectural assets, not ADM process.

Answer Choice C) To describe how an architecture addresses stakeholder concerns : Done as part of ADM, especially in Phase A onwards. Enterprise Continuum is only about architectural assets, not ADM process.

Answer Choice D) To evaluate how best to develop and implement an architecture : Done as part of ADM, especially in Phase E and Phase F. Enterprise Continuum is only about architectural assets, not ADM process.

Answer Choice E) To help identify and understand business requirements : Done as part of ADM, especially in Phase B. Enterprise Continuum is only about architectural assets, not ADM process.

Answer : A

Q 1317 Which one of the following is the most generic artifact in the Architecture Continuum ?

A. Common Systems Architecture

B. Foundation Architecture

C. Industry Architecture

D. Organization Specific Architecture

E. Product Line Architecture

Explanation :

Foundation Architecture, naturally, is most generic artifact in the Architecture Continuum.

See under : **6.4.1 Architecture Continuum : Foundation Architecture**[31]

A Foundation Architecture consists ..., and ..

The TOGAF® ADM is a ... of such .. in order to create ..

The ... is an example of a ...

It is a ... upon which ... can be based.

Also see under : **6.3 Constituents of the Enterprise Continuum**[32]

The Architecture Continuum is ... to discover ...

This is why the Foundation Architecture occupies left-most and top-most corner position in it.

---

31. https://pubs.opengroup.org/togaf-standard/architecture-content/chap06.html#tag_06_04_01_01

32. https://pubs.opengroup.org/togaf-standard/architecture-content/chap06.html#tag_06_03

Product Line Architecture, which is more of PLM (Product Lifecycle Management) is only a type of architectural horizontal and is never generic.

Answer : B

Q 1318 Which of the following best completes the sentence: The Enterprise Continuum _____

A. describes a database of open industry standards

B. is an architecture framework

C. is a technical reference model

D. provides a method for architecture development

E. provides methods for classifying artifacts

Explanation :

The Enterprise Continuum is a model providing methods for classifying architecture and solution artifacts as they evolve from generic Foundation Architectures to Organization-Specific Architectures. The Enterprise Continuum comprises two complementary concepts : the Architecture Continuum and the Solutions Continuum.

See : **1.4 Introduction**[33] (to Enterprise Continuum) : 1. Introduction : under Architecture Content part of TOGAF® Standard Fundamental Content Version 10

The Enterprise Continuum describes view of the Architecture Repository that provides methods for classifying architecture and solution artifacts, showing how the different types of artifact evolve, and how they can be leveraged and re-used. It is usually impossible to create a single unified architecture that meets all requirements of all stakeholders for all time. Therefore, the Enterprise Architect will need to deal not just with a single Enterprise Architecture, but with many related Enterprise Architectures.

Each architecture will .... another. Effectively .... is therefore a .... in allowing architects to .... problem space ... that can be .... The Enterprise Continuum provides .... Repository that shows the ... from ..., from ..., and from ...

Answer Choice A) describes a database of open industry standards : Only Industry Architecture portion of Enterprise Continuum.

Answer Choice B) is an architecture framework : There are many architecture frameworks and also EAF – Enterprise Architecture Frameworks. But Enterprise Continuum is not a framework by itself. It is part of TOGAF® which is an EAF.

Answer Choice C) is a technical reference model : TRM is a technical reference model recommended by TOGAF® and so is usually just a part of Enterprise Continuum.

Answer Choice D) provides a method for architecture development : This is about ADM, which is a different component of TOGAF®, just as Enterprise Continuum being a component.

---

33. https://pubs.opengroup.org/togaf-standard/architecture-content/chap01.html#tag_01_04

Answer : E

_____

Q 1319 Complete the sentence : The architectures that address the detailed enterprise needs and business requirements within the Architecture Continuum are known as_____

A. Strategic Architectures

B. Foundation Architectures

C. Industry Architectures

D. Common Systems Architectures

E. Organization-Specific Architectures

Explanation :

Organization-Specific Architectures are viewed as being at the right end of the Architecture Continuum and are the most relevant to the IT customer community since they describe and guide the final architecture that is meant for the deployment of solution components for a particular Enterprise or extended network of connected Enterprises.

See : **6.4.1 Architecture Continuum : Organization-Specific Architectures**[34] :

Organization-Specific Architectures describe and guide ... for a .. or ....

There may be a ... that are needed to ... by ....

Alternatively, this might result in ... for specific .... : What are the level of details mentioned here ?

The Organization-Specific Architecture ..., and has the following characteristics :

▪ Provides ... ▪ Reflects ... ▪ Defines ...

▪ Contains ... ▪ Provides ... ▪ Provides ...

▪ Provides ...

Read the explanation appearing under **Q 1304**

Answer : E

_____

Q 1320 According to TOGAF®, which one of the following is described as a view of the Architecture Repository and provides methods for classifying architecture and solution artifacts as they evolve ?

A. Architecture Landscape

B. Architecture Governance Repository

---

34. https://pubs.opengroup.org/togaf-standard/architecture-content/chap06.html#tag_06_04_01_04

C. Enterprise Continuum

D. Governance Repository

E. Standards Information Base

Explanation :

See : **1.4 Introduction**[35] (to Enterprise Continuum) : 1. Introduction : under Architecture Content part of TOGAF® Standard Fundamental Content Version 10

The Enterprise Continuum provides .... that shows the evolution of these related ... from ... to ..., from .. to .., and from ... to ....

Each ... will have a ... and ... will relate to ....

Effectively bounding the scope of an ... therefore a ... in allowing .... to .. a .. into .. that can be .... addressed

The Enterprise Continuum describes a view of the Architecture Repository that provides methods for classifying architecture and solution artifacts, showing how the different types of artifact evolve, and how they can be leveraged and reused.

Answer Choice A) Architecture Landscape D) Governance Repository and E) Standards Information Base : these are indeed portions of Architecture repository. What is contained in a Repository cannot be a 'view' of the same.

On Answer Choice B) Architecture Governance Repository : See **1.4 Architecture Governance**[36] : 1. Introduction under Architecture Development Method part of TOGAF® Standard Fundamental Content Version 10

The task of managing all architectural artifact assets, as also that of governing through control of related processes needs a system by itself. Naturally this demand one or more repositories and a indexed way of accessing it. Hence we need an Enterprise Continuum system which will describe a view of the Repository supporting versioned objects, process control, and status.

Hence this will be part of Architecture Repository. It can alternatively be a separate one as chosen by the Tailored TOGAF® for the Enterprise.

Answer : C

Q 1321 Does not apply to Common System Solution

A. Represents the highest common denominator for one or more solutions in the industry segments that the Common Systems Solution supports

B. Can comprise of Industry Specific Architectures that is common only to a few industries

C. Provide organizations with operating environments specific to operational and informational needs

---

35. https://pubs.opengroup.org/togaf-standard/architecture-content/chap01.html#tag_01_04

36. https://pubs.opengroup.org/togaf-standard/adm/chap01.html#tag_01_04

D. Examples include high availability transaction processing and scalable data warehousing systems

Explanation :

Industry Architectures guide the integration of common systems components. Common Systems Architectures **cannot** comprise of Industry Specific Architectures that is common only to a few industries.

See under : **6.4.1 Architecture Continuum**[37]

Common Systems Architectures

Common Systems Architectures guide the ...... and .... of specific services from the .... to create an .... common (i.e., ...) solutions across a ... relevant .... : Take 'relevant domains' as ones that cover something among B, D, A, T as also their highly reusable common areas such as Authentication mechanisms, Authorization mechanisms, User interface dialogues for File Opening, File Saving, Choosing form an enumerated regulars such as Colour selection, Choosing fields from a Data schema for 'Select' style retrieval, configuring varieties of hardware and Infrastructure situation and so on.

It can also be ones for SNMP – Simple Network Managing Protocol related system management areas, for provisioning in the Cloud, Converting report format, say from .docx to pdf and such commonly needed format conversion, converting from dataset of a specific database (SQL, No-SQL) into XML or JSON and so on.

Also see the examples given by TOGAF® :

Examples of Common Systems Architectures include: a ... architecture, a ... architecture, a .... architecture, an ... architecture, etc. Each is incomplete in .... but is complete in terms of a ... (...., ..., ..., ..., etc.), so that .... the architecture ... re-usable.

Industry Architectures

Industry Architectures guide the ....of .... components with industry specific ...and guide the creation of .... for targeted .... within a particular industry : See how these in turn make use of Common systems but do extend the architecture into areas very specific to that industry. Say, in case of Banking Industry, it could be for branch banking process, loan application and sanctioning processes and so on. In case of Travel Industry, it could be for booking and reservation, selection of right travel product or service among the alternatives and so on.

Answer : B

Q 1322 In the Solutions Continuum, which of the following is the correct order of Solutions from most specific to most-generic ?

A. Common Systems, Foundation, Industry, Organization-Specific

B. Organization-Specific, Industry, Foundation, Common Systems

C. Foundation, Common Systems, Industry, Organization-Specific

---

37. https://pubs.opengroup.org/togaf-standard/architecture-content/chap06.html#tag_06_04_01

D. Industry, Foundation, Common Systems, Organization-Specific

E. Organization-Specific, Industry, Common Systems, Foundation

Explanation :

In Solutions Continuum the correct order of Solutions going from most specific to most-generic happens to be : Organization-Specific, Industry, Common Systems, Foundation.

See under : **6.4.2 Solutions Continuum**[38]

"Moving to the left" on the Solutions Continuum ... on .... This matches the correct answer, when we have to move Solutions from most specific to most-generic.

"Moving to the right" on the Solutions Continuum is focused on ... (i.e., ...).

See : **Figure 6-1**[39] Enterprise Continuum and the text below that

- The **Enterprise Continuum** is the ... and ...

- The **Architecture Continuum** offers ... relationships (e.g., ...)

- The **Solutions Continuum** provides ... defined in the Architecture Continuum

Answer : E

Q 1323 Which of the following statements is not correct about Enterprise Continuum ?

A. It is a view of the Architecture Repository that provides methods for classifying architecture and solution artifacts, both internal and external to the Architecture Repository

B. It is an important aid to communication and understanding, both within individual enterprises, and between customer enterprises and vendor organizations

C. It also represents an aid to organizing re-usable architecture and solution assets

D. It is a physical repository of all architecture assets models, patterns, architecture descriptions, and other artifacts produced during application of the ADM

E. It represents an aid to communication

Explanation :

Enterprise Continuum is not a physical repository. It is a virtual one.

See : **6.1 Overview** [40]

---

38. https://pubs.opengroup.org/togaf-standard/architecture-content/chap06.html#tag_06_04_02

39. https://pubs.opengroup.org/togaf-standard/architecture-content/chap06.html#tagfcjh_12

40. https://pubs.opengroup.org/togaf-standard/architecture-content/chap06.html#tag_06_01

The Enterprise Continuum provides methods for classifying ... and ... artifacts, both .... and ... to the Architecture Repository, as they evolve from .... to ... : It is an indexed classification mechanism (for accessing) both ABB based architecture assets and SBB based solution artifacts. Point to note is about the 'evolution' path mentioned here, and you can note that it goes from left to right in the images shown.

The Enterprise Continuum enables the architect to ... of .... the Enterprise Architecture has been ... with the ... considered : What is the articulation expected ?

The Enterprise Continuum is an important ...., both within ..., and between ... and ... : Important for what ?

Without an understanding of "...", people discussing architecture can often talk at .... because they are ... in the ... at the ..., without ...it : Provides for a uniform way for everyone to look into the architectural contents. The Repository schema may not distinguish between Fundamental content, Common System as a grouped re-usable sub-system content, the ones that came for Industry specific sources and finally what we have produced in our Enterprise as ultimately accepted solutions for each Portfolio and its Transition Architecture. On the other hand Enterprise Continuum does exactly the same that is needed for uniform access.

Answer : D

Q 1324 Which among the following statements about Architecture Continuum is NOT true ?

A. It offers a consistent way to define and understand the generic rules, representations, and relationships in an architecture, including traceability and derivation relationships

B. It represents a structuring of Architecture Building Blocks (ABBs) which are re-usable architecture assets

C. The relationship between the Architecture Continuum and the Solutions Continuum is not to be mistaken as one of guidance, direction, and support.

D. It shows the relationships among foundational frameworks, common system architectures, industry architectures, and enterprise architectures

E. It is a useful tool to discover commonality and eliminate unnecessary redundancy

Explanation :

There is **no stipulation** in TOGAF® that for every single Building Block of ABB appearing in the Architecture Continuum, there **has to be a** corresponding SBB Building Block in the Solutions Continuum. There is **no need to have Block to Block correspondence**. Do not mistake this with general relationship between the two Continuums where Solution Continuum is stated to have one to one correspondence with four such levels of the Architecture Continuum. This statement is about Level to Level correspondence.

See : **6.6.1 Relationships**[41] :

The relationship between the ... and the ... is **one of guidance, direction, and support**.

Each of the three continua contains . about the... .... of the architectures during their ... : Why three ? It counts the superset of Enterprise Continuum along with the two subsets of Architecture Continuum and Solutions Continuum.

- The Enterprise Continuum provides an overall context for ..... and .... that apply across the ...... of the enterprise : Overall context for what ? Where do they apply ?

- The Architecture Continuum provides a classification mechanism for .... that .. the architecture at .... of evolution from ... : What is this mechanism ? Why 'collectively define' ?

- The Solutions Continuum provides the ..... for assets to describe ... for the .... that can be implemented to .... the ... of the architecture : To achieve what ? Is the word 'organization' here is about the Enterprise or a department ?

The relationship between the Architecture Continuum and the Solutions Continuum is one of ...., ..., and .. For example, ... guide the ...or .. of .... Solutions. ..... support the .... Architecture by helping to realize the ... in the Architecture Continuum : Definition is important. Example is nice to read.

The .... Architecture also guides development of ... Solutions, by providing ...., ... and .. that guide ..., and ... of appropriate solutions. A similar relationship exists between the ..... of the Enterprise Continuum. The Enterprise Continuum should not be ..... as representing ..... Organization-Specific Architectures could have components from a ..... Architecture, and Organization-Specific Solutions could contain ... : What is provided, by what ? What is the "similar relationship" situations motioned ? What is the wrong interpretation cautioned against here ?

Answer : C

Q 1325 The relationship between the Architecture Continuum and the Solutions Continuum is one of ___ (complete the sentence).

A. Guidance, derivation and support

B. Guidance, direction and support

C. Governance, direction and support

D. Guidance, direction and supplementing

E. Governance, derivation and supplementing

Explanation :

The relationship between the ... and the ... is one that involves ....

Guidance : Anytime that a solution artifact needs a basic explanation, look for it in the Architecture Continuum.

Derivation : You might find a abstract ABB for the concrete SBB.

Support : Hence use these to explain the architectural output and have a supporting concept as seen in the Architecture Continuum. Challenges can be

See : **6.6.1 Relationships**[42] :

The relationship between the Architecture Continuum and the Solutions Continuum ....

For example, ...

Foundation Solutions ...

The Foundation Architecture also guides ..., by ... that guide .. of ....

A similar relationship exists between ....

The Enterprise Continuum ... through leverage.

The Architecture Continuum ....

The Solutions Continuum offers a ....

Refer to explanation appearing under **Q 1324**

Answer : B

Q 1326 Complete the sentence. According to TOGAF®, the simplest way of thinking about the Enterprise Continuum is as a _____

A. Configuration Database

B. Library of architecture artifacts

C. Requirements Management System

D. Standards Information Base

E. View of the Architecture Repository

Explanation :

In simple terms, Enterprise Continuum is a (virtual) view of the Architecture Repository.

See : **3.10 Enterprise Continuum**[43] : 3. Core Concepts under Introduction and Core Concepts part of TOGAF® Standard Fundamental Content Version 10

... which sets the ..... for an architect and ...... how ....and .... in order to support ...... : Has a broad spectrum context (all content of the Enterprise, from present projects back to all earlier ones, as also many third party references and standards); leveraging meaning taking advantage of generic solutions – ABBs.

The Enterprise Continuum is a view of the Architecture Repository that provides .... Architectures.

EC, Enterprise Continuum is closely related to this Component of TOGAF®.

EC, Enterprise Continuum is closely related to this Component of TOGAF®.

42. https://pubs.opengroup.org/togaf-standard/architecture-content/chap06.html#tag_06_06_01

43. https://pubs.opengroup.org/togaf-standard/introduction/chap03.html#tag_03_10

Answer Choice A) Configuration Database : This is about CMDB – Configuration Management Data Base, which is separate repository. See it being placed outside Enterprise Continuum in **Figure 3-4**[44] : **3.10 Enterprise Continuum**[45] : 3. Core Concepts under Introduction and Core Concepts part of TOGAF® Standard Fundamental Content Version 10

Answer Choice B) Library of architecture artifacts : Is part of Architecture Repository. Enterprise Continuum is only a 'view' of the same.

Answer Choice C) Requirements Management System : is part of ADM, which is separate (but related) component of TOGAF® as compared to Enterprise Continuum.

Answer Choice D) Standards Information Base : Is part of Architecture Repository. Enterprise Continuum is only a 'view' of the same.

Answer : E

Q 1327 In the Solutions Continuum, which of the following is the correct order of solutions ranging from generic solution to enterprise specific solution ?

A. Foundation, Common Systems, Industry, Organization-Specific

B. Industry, Foundation, Common Systems, Organization-Specific

C. Organization-Specific, Industry, Common Systems, Foundation

D. Organization-Specific, Industry, Foundation, Common Systems

Explanation :

Correct order, of solutions ranging from generic solution to enterprise specific solution is : Foundation, Common Systems, Industry, Organization-Specific.

See under : **6.4.2 Solutions Continuum**[46]

"Moving to the right" on the Solutions Continuum is ... (i.e., ... create ...).

Foundation Solutions : .. are ... that are the ...

Common Systems Solutions : ... is an implementation of ... comprised of ..., which may be ..

Industry Solutions : ... is an implementation of ..., which provides ... specific to ..

Organization-Specific Solutions : ... is an implementation of the ... that provides the ....

Because solutions are designed for ..., they contain ... in order to ...

---

44. https://pubs.opengroup.org/togaf-standard/introduction/chap03.html#tagfcjh_8

45. https://pubs.opengroup.org/togaf-standard/introduction/chap03.html#tag_03_10

46. https://pubs.opengroup.org/togaf-standard/architecture-content/chap06.html#tag_06_04_02

No need to repeat that this kind of ordering is pretty important. It makes sense to learn more about Each sub-Component of the Continuum.

Answer : A

Q 1328

Complete the sentence. The Architecture Development Method produces content to be stored in the Repository, which is classified according to the _____.

A. ADM Guidelines and Techniques

B. Architecture Capability Framework

C. Enterprise Continuum

D. Standards Information Base

Explanation :

All content stored in the Architecture Repository is classified (indexed) according to the Enterprise Continuum.

See under : **1.4 Architecture Governance**[47] : 1. Introduction under Architecture Development Method part of TOGAF® Standard Fundamental Content Version 10

The ADM, ... or used as ..., is a ... in the same manner as ... and held in the ....

ADM, Architecture Repository and this : Three have a close relationship.

Answer Choice A) ADM Guidelines and Techniques : Not an architecture content, but consumes and produces one.

Answer Choice B) Architecture Capability Framework : Is about improving capability of the Enterprise and more about Governance content and not architecture artifact content.

Answer Choice D) Standards Information Base – SIB : Not produced by ADM. It is consumed during ADM process when a need to lookup for a specific standard arises.

Answer : C

Q 1329 Which of the following in the Enterprise Continuum is an example of an internal architecture or solution artifact that is available for re-use ?

A. Deliverables from previous architecture work

B. Industry reference models and patterns

C. The TOGAF® TRM

D. The TOGAF® III-RM

Explanation :

Deliverables (and other artifacts) from previous architecture work, such as previous ADM cycles are internal architecture which have reached the solution stage. These are available for re-use.

On other incorrect Answer Choices, these being not 'internal architectures' but being produced elsewhere :

Answer Choice B) Industry reference models and patterns : these are picked from industry sources and best practice recommendations from outside the Enterprise.

Answer Choices C) and D) The TOGAF® TRM : As the name implies, it is provided by TOGAF® as a reference library. The TOGAF® III-RM is a reference model that supports describing Common Systems Architecture in the Application Domain that focuses on the requirements, Building Blocks, and standards relating to the concept of Boundaryless Information Flow™. Refer to **6.4 Enterprise Continuum in Detail**[48] for more

Answer : A

Q 1330 Which of the following best completes the next sentence: The Enterprise Continuum aids communication

A. Within enterprises

B. Between enterprises

C. With vendor organizations

D. By providing a consistent language to communicate the differences between architectures

E. All of these

Explanation :

The Enterprise Continuum does aid communication within single enterprise, between enterprises, with vendor organizations, It provides a consistent language to communicate the differences between architectures.

See : **6.1 Overview** [49]

The Enterprise Continuum provides ..... and drivers considered.

The Enterprise Continuum ... and vendor organizations.

Without an understanding of "..", people discussing architecture can ... without realizing it. : When will it lead to cross-proposes ?

Also to note from : **6.2 Enterprise Continuum and Architecture Re-Use**[50] : : Important set of points.

---

48. https://pubs.opengroup.org/togaf-standard/architecture-content/chap06.html#tag_06_04

49. https://pubs.opengroup.org/togaf-standard/architecture-content/chap06.html#tag_06_01

The simplest way of ... is as a ....

It can contain ..., and other artifacts — that exist both ..., which the enterprise considers ...

The 'between' in Answer Choice B) is to be taken as : The Enterprise Continuum is .. to communication ..., both ..., and between ...**enterprises** and ... **organizations.**

Answer : E

Q 1331 Which of the following are considered to be the constituent parts of the Enterprise Continuum ?

A. Standards Information Base, Governance Repository

B. TOGAF® TRM, III-RM

C. Architecture Continuum, Solutions Continuum

D. Business Architecture, Application Architecture

Explanation :

Architecture Continuum, Solutions Continuum are the only two constituent parts of Enterprise Continuum. **Do not mistake** any constituent part of Architecture Repository to be a constituent part of Enterprise Continuum.

Architecture Repository is **based on storage schema**. Enterprise Continuum is **based on retrieval schema**.

But it contains many things, as seen in **6.2 Enterprise Continuum and Architecture Re-Use[51]** :

The simplest way of ... is as a ....

It can contain ..., and other artifacts — that exist both ..., which the enterprise considers ...

Examples of ... and ... are the ..., which are ....

Examples of .. and .. are the ... and .. that ..., and are ..., including those that are .. (such as ...the TOGAF® TRM); those specific to ...(such as ...); those specific to .., such as .., etc.; and those specific to .., such as the ... etc.

The Enterprise Architecture determines ....

Re-use is a ....

On Answer Choice A) Standards Information Base, Governance Repository : These are part of Architecture Repository.

On Answer Choice B) The TOGAF® TRM is an example of a Foundation Architecture. It is a fundamental architecture upon which other, more specific architectures can be based. The TOGAF® Integrated Information Infrastructure Reference Model (III-RM) is a reference model that supports describing Common Systems Architecture in the Application Domain that focuses on the requirements, Building Blocks, and standards relating to the vision of

---

50. https://pubs.opengroup.org/togaf-standard/architecture-content/chap06.html#tag_06_02

51. https://pubs.opengroup.org/togaf-standard/architecture-content/chap06.html#tag_06_02

Boundaryless Information Flow™. These are also part of Architecture Repository, if these happen to be reference models stored therein. .

On Answer Choice D) Business Architecture, Application Architecture : These are phases of ADM.

Answer : C

––––––––––––––

Q 1332 Which of the following statements is true : The TOGAF® Integrated Information Infrastructure Reference Model is classified in the Architecture Continuum as :

A. An example of a Common Systems Architecture

B. An example of an Industry Architecture

C. An example of an Enterprise Architecture

D. An example of a Foundation Architecture

Explanation :

The III-RM is a Common Systems Architecture. It connects Information Providers and Information Consumers (who are two different systems) through a common Broker system.

See under **6.4.1 Architecture Continuum : Common Systems Architectures**[52]

Common Systems Architectures ... from the ... to create .. (i.e., ..) solutions across ....

Examples of Common Systems Architectures include : ....

The ... is a reference model that supports describing Common Systems Architecture in the ... that focuses on ... relating to the ...

Answer Choices, which are not true in this question context of III-RM are :

For Answer Choice B) : An example of an Industry Architecture : See under **6.4.1 Architecture Continuum : Industry Architectures**[53]

A typical example of an industry-specific component is ..., such as the ..., or an ..

For Answer Choice C) : An example of an Enterprise Architecture, we can take TOGAF® itself.

For Answer Choice D) : An example of a Foundation Architecture ; We can take TRM.

Answer : A

Q 1333 Which of the following responses does not complete the next sentence ? The Solutions Continuum

––––––––––––––––––––––

52. https://pubs.opengroup.org/togaf-standard/architecture-content/chap06.html#tag_06_04_01_02

53. https://pubs.opengroup.org/togaf-standard/architecture-content/chap06.html#tag_06_04_01_03

A. Provides a way to understand the implementation of assets defined in the Architecture Continuum

B. Addresses the commonalities and differences among the products, systems, and services of an implemented system

C. Can be considered to have at each level a set of Building Blocks that represent a solution to the business requirements at that level

D. Contains a number of re-usable Architecture Building Blocks

E. Has a relationship to the Architecture Continuum that includes guidance, direction, and support

Explanation :

ABBs are part of the Architecture Continuum. So, they will not be part of Solutions Continuum.

See under : **6.3 Constituents of the Enterprise Continuum**[54]

▪ The **Solutions Continuum** provides ... defined in the Architecture Continuum

The Solutions Continuum defines ... as ....

The solutions are the ... between .. that ... defined in ....

The Solutions Continuum addresses ... among the of implemented products, systems, and services system.....

Also see : **6.4.2 Solutions Continuum**[55]

The Solutions Continuum represents ... at the .... At each level, the

Solutions Continuum is a ... with reference ... that represent .. expressed at ....

A populated repository based on the Solutions Continuum can be regarded ..., which can ...

Answer : D

Q 1334 Which one of the following category of reference Building Blocks is not part of the Solutions Continuum ?

A. Systems libraries

B. Organization-specific solutions

C. Foundation solutions

D. Common systems solutions

E. Industry solutions

Explanation :

54. https://pubs.opengroup.org/togaf-standard/architecture-content/chap06.html#tag_06_03

55. https://pubs.opengroup.org/togaf-standard/architecture-content/chap06.html#tag_06_04_02

Libraries of Architectural content (Systems libraries) are pure reference material which can help us build the ABB. It cannot be part of Solutions Continuum directly since it falls short of giving specific solution to the problem at hand.

See under : **6.4.2 Solutions Continuum**[56] and in **Figure 6-3**[57]

The following subsections describe ... types within the ...

Foundation Solutions : ... are ...

Common Systems Solutions : .. is an ...

Industry Solutions : ... is an implementation of ...

Organization-Specific Solutions : ... is an implementation of ...

Answer : A

──────────

Q 1335 Which of the following is considered a model for a physical instance of the Enterprise Continuum ?

A. The Architecture Repository

B. The III-RM

C. The Standards Information Base

D. The TOGAF® TRM

Explanation :

The Architecture Repository is considered a model for a physical instance of the Enterprise Continuum. In other words, a logical view of Architecture Repository is Enterprise Continuum. But note that Enterprise Continuum may refer to more resources than that is physically stored in Architecture Repository. It can refer to external pointers also.

See : **6.1 Overview** [58]:

The Enterprise Continuum provides .., both ... to the .., as they evolve from ...

Also see : **6.2 Enterprise Continuum and Architecture Re-Use**[59] :

The simplest way of thinking of the Enterprise Continuum is as a .... for the enterprise.

On incorrect answer choices :

Answer Choice B) The III-RM : A Common Systems Architecture which is in the Architecture Continuum part of Enterprise Continuum.

---

56. https://pubs.opengroup.org/togaf-standard/architecture-content/chap06.html#tag_06_04_02

57. https://pubs.opengroup.org/togaf-standard/architecture-content/chap06.html#tagfcjh_14

58. https://pubs.opengroup.org/togaf-standard/architecture-content/chap06.html#tag_06_01

59. https://pubs.opengroup.org/togaf-standard/architecture-content/chap06.html#tag_06_02

Answer Choice C) The Standards Information Base : One of the six parts of Architecture Repository.

Answer Choice D) The TOGAF® TRM : A Foundation Architecture which is in the Architecture Continuum part of Enterprise Continuum.

Answer : A

———————————

Q 1336 The difference between the two portions of Enterprise Continuum, Architecture Continuum and Solutions Continuum is

A. First one is Strategic and second one is Segmental

B. First one is for EA and second one is for Solutions Architecture

C. First one is for Vision Phase and second is for other Phases

D. First one is conceptual functionality only whereas the second one is implementable assets

Explanation :

In Enterprise Continuum :

Architecture Continuum is conceptual functionality only (ABB)

Solution continuum is one implementable assets (SBB)

See : **6.6.1 Relationships**[60] : Each of the . contains .... about the .. during their lifecycle :

▪ The Enterprise Continuum provides ..

▪ The Architecture Continuum provides ...

▪ The Solutions Continuum provides ..

Answer Choices which are not part of Enterprise Continuum :

Answer Choice A) First one is Strategic and second one is Segmental : These are kinds of Architectural Partition. See **4. Architecture Partitioning**[61] under Applying the ADM part of TOGAF® Standard Fundamental Content Version 10

Answer Choice B) First one is for EA and second one is for Solutions Architecture : These are kind of Architectures.

See : **4.72 Solution Architecture**[62] and

See **1.1 Executive Overview**[63] under Introduction and Core Concepts part of TOGAF® Standard Fundamental Content Version 10

---

60. https://pubs.opengroup.org/togaf-standard/architecture-content/chap06.html#tag_06_06_01

61. https://pubs.opengroup.org/togaf-standard/applying-the-adm/chap04.html

62. https://pubs.opengroup.org/togaf-standard/introduction/chap04.html#tag_04_72

63. https://pubs.opengroup.org/togaf-standard/introduction/chap01.html#tag_01_01

Answer Choice C) First one is for Vision Phase and second is for other Phases : These relate to Phases of ADM. Phases of ADM only have a producer - consumer equation with Enterprise Continuum, that too through the Architecture Repository. Not easy to pin down a phase to a part of Enterprise Continuum.

Answer : D

Q 1337 According to TOGAF®, which of the following best describes how the Enterprise Continuum is used in organizing and developing an architecture ?

A. It is used to coordinate with the other management frameworks in use

B. It is used to describe how an architecture addresses stakeholder concerns

C. It is used to identify and understand business requirements

D. It is used to provide a system for continuous monitoring

E. It is used to structure re-usable architecture and solution assets

Explanation :

Enterprise Continuum is used to structure re-usable architecture and solution assets in the process of organizing and developing an architecture.

See under : **6.1 Overview** [64]:

The Enterprise Continuum enables ... opportunities.

Answer Choice A) It is used to coordinate with the other management frameworks in use : Done as part of ADM, especially in Phase F. Enterprise Continuum is only about architectural assets, not ADM process.

Answer Choice B) It is used to describe how an architecture addresses stakeholder concerns : Done as part of ADM, especially in Phase A onwards. Enterprise Continuum is only about architectural assets, not ADM process.

Answer Choice C) It is used to identify and understand business requirements : Done as part of ADM, especially in Phase B. Enterprise Continuum is only about architectural assets, not ADM process.

Answer Choice D) It is used to provide a system for continuous monitoring : Architecture Contract and many other Governance artifacts are used here and they may not be part of Enterprise Continuum.

See **5.1 Role** [65] : 5. Architecture Contracts : Enterprise Architecture Capability and Governance part of TOGAF® Standard Fundamental Content Version 10

• A system of ... within the organization

Answer : E

---

64. https://pubs.opengroup.org/togaf-standard/architecture-content/chap06.html#tag_06_01

65. https://pubs.opengroup.org/togaf-standard/ea-capability-and-governance/chap05.html#tag_05_01

Q 1338 Complete the sentence : Building Blocks that are viewed as being at the left-hand side of the Solutions Continuum are known as _____.

A. Common Systems Solutions

B. Foundation Solutions

C. Industry Solutions

D. Organization-Specific Solutions

E. Strategic Solutions

Explanation :

Foundations Solutions get placed on the left-hand side of the Solutions Continuum; actually, it is the left most.

See under : **6.4.2 Solutions Continuum**[66]

"Moving to the right" on the Solutions Continuum ... (i.e., ... solutions).

"Moving to the left" on the Solutions Continuum is ....

These two viewpoints are ... leverage.

Answer : B

Q 1339 Complete the sentence. The Enterprise Continuum provides methods for classifying architecture artifacts as they evolve from _____ _____

A. Foundation Architectures to re-usable architecture assets

B. Generic Architectures to Organization-Specific Architectures

C. Generic Solutions to Industry Models

D. Generic architectures to reusable Solution Building Blocks

E. Solutions Architectures to Solution Building Blocks

Explanation :

In Enterprise Continuum artifacts evolve from generic (Foundation) architectures to Organization-Specific Architectures. The in between ones are Common Systems and Industry Specific Architectures.

See : **6.1 Overview**[67]

The Enterprise Continuum provides ... Architectures.

---

66. https://pubs.opengroup.org/togaf-standard/architecture-content/chap06.html#tag_06_04_02

67. https://pubs.opengroup.org/togaf-standard/architecture-content/chap06.html#tag_06_01

Answer Choice A) Foundation Architectures to re-usable architecture assets : **Not an evolution**. TOGAF® expects all artifacts to be re-usable

Answer Choice C) Generic solutions to Industry Models : Actually the **evolution is from** Foundation to Organization (Enterprise) specific

Answer Choice D) Generic Architectures to reusable Solution Building Blocks : **Not an evolution**. TOGAF® expects all artifacts to be re-usable

Answer Choice E) Solutions Architectures to Solution Building Blocks : **All are Building Blocks**. We are talking in this question on methods for classifying architecture artifacts as they evolve

Answer : B

Q 1340 Spot the wrong statement

A. The TOGAF® TRM is an example of a Foundation Solution. It is an architecture upon which other, more specific architectures can be based

B. A typical example of an industry-specific component is a data model representing the business functions and processes specific to a particular vertical industry, such as the Retail industry's "Active Store" architecture, or an Industry Architecture that incorporates the Energistics Data Model

C. Example Foundation Solutions would include programming languages, operating systems, foundational data structures (such as EDIFACT), generic approaches to organization structuring, foundational structures for organizing IT operations (such as ITIL or the IT4IT Reference Architecture), etc.,

D. Any architecture is context-specific; for example, there are architectures that are specific to individual customers, industries, subsystems, products, and services

Explanation :

Examples cited in Answer Choices B) C) and D) are appropriate for corresponding sections in Enterprise Continuum.

Answer Choice A) is one of Foundation Architecture, **not Foundation Solution**. That is why it is wrong statement.

Referring to TOGAF® documentation for the 'true' Answer Choices :

Answer Choice B) : under **6.2 Enterprise Continuum and Architecture Re-Use :**[68] Those specific to certain ..., such as the ... like the .. (in the .. sector), .. (...), .. (..), etc.,

Answer Choice C) : under 6.4.2 Solutions Continuum : See **Foundation Solutions**[69]

Answer Choice D) : under **6.1 Overview**[70]

Answer : A

68. https://pubs.opengroup.org/togaf-standard/architecture-content/chap06.html#tag_06_02

69. https://pubs.opengroup.org/togaf-standard/architecture-content/chap06.html#tag_06_04_02_01

70. https://pubs.opengroup.org/togaf-standard/architecture-content/chap06.html#tag_06_01

Q 1341 Which of the following statements about Enterprise Continuum is NOT correct ?

A. It is a physical repository of all architecture assets models, patterns, architecture descriptions, and other artifacts produced during application of the ADM

B. It is a view of the Architecture Repository that provides methods for classifying architecture and solution artifacts, both internal and external to the Architecture Repository

C. It is an important aid to communication and understanding, both within individual enterprises, and between customer enterprises and vendor organizations

D. It also leads to organizing re-usable architecture and solution assets

E. It represents an aid to communication

Explanation :

Note that Architectural Repository is the physical one. **Enterprise Continuum is a logical (virtual) index** to what is in Architecture Repository and also to relevant external resources.

Referring to TOGAF® documentation for the 'true' Answer Choices :

Answer Choice B) It is a view of the Architecture Repository that provides methods for classifying architecture and solution artifacts, both internal and external to the Architecture Repository

Answer Choice C) It is an important aid to communication and understanding, both within individual enterprises, and between customer enterprises and vendor organizations : See under **6.1 Overview**[71]

Answer Choice D) It also represents an aid to organizing re-usable architecture and solution assets :

See under : **6.2 Enterprise Continuum and Architecture Re-Use**[72] : The Enterprise Architecture determines ... this decision.

Answer Choice E) It represents an aid to communication : See under **6.1 Overview**[73]

Answer : A

Q 1342 Where is the TOGAF® Technical Reference Model positioned in terms of the Enterprise Continuum ?

A. The left-hand side of the Architecture Continuum

B. The right-hand side of the Architecture Continuum

C. The left-hand side of the Solutions Continuum

71. https://pubs.opengroup.org/togaf-standard/architecture-content/chap06.html#tag_06_01

72. https://pubs.opengroup.org/togaf-standard/architecture-content/chap06.html#tag_06_02

73. https://pubs.opengroup.org/togaf-standard/architecture-content/chap06.html#tag_06_01

D. The right-hand side of the Solutions Continuum

Explanation :

It is at the left-hand side, the most generic, of the Architecture.

See : **6.4.1 Architecture Continuum**[74]

The Architecture Continuum .... Organization-Specific Architectures.

The arrows ... and Building Blocks.

The enterprise ... for their business.

Also see : **Figure 6-2 Architecture Continuum**[75]

Answer : A

Q 1343 How is the III-RM classified in terms of the Enterprise Continuum ?

A. Industry Solution

B. Foundation Architecture

C. Common Systems Architecture

D. Common Systems Solution

Explanation :

III-RM connects two sides of interoperability (SOA) as a common system. Connects, as Broker, between the two systems of Information Provider and Information Consumer.

See under : **6.4.1 Architecture Continuum : Common Systems Architectures**[76]

Common Systems Architectures ....across a wide number of relevant domains.

Examples of Common Systems Architectures include : ... operating states of the enterprise.

The ... is a reference model that supports .....

Answer : C

Q 1344 Complete the sentence. The Solutions Continuum represents implementations of the architectures at corresponding levels of _____.

74. https://pubs.opengroup.org/togaf-standard/architecture-content/chap06.html#tag_06_04_01

75. https://pubs.opengroup.org/togaf-standard/architecture-content/chap06.html#tagfcjh_13

76. https://pubs.opengroup.org/togaf-standard/architecture-content/chap06.html#tag_06_04_01_02

A. Architecture Capability

B. Architecture Continuum

C. Architecture Landscape

D. Architecture Metamodel

E. Architecture Repository

Explanation :

Solutions Continuum has one to one correspondence with four such levels of the Architecture Continuum.

See : **6.4.2 Solutions Continuum**[77]

The Solutions Continuum represents .... improvements to the enterprise.

See under : **6.6.1 Relationships**[78]

The relationship between the ... other elements of the Enterprise Continuum.

Also see : **Figure 6-4 : Relationships between Architecture and Solutions Continua**[79]

Answer : B

———————

FOLLOWING POINTS MAY require attention at this stage :

Although all of the TOGAF® documentation works together as a whole, it is expected that organizations will customize it during adoption, and deliberately choose some elements, customize some, exclude some, and create others. For example, an organization may wish to adopt the TOGAF® metamodel, but elect not to use any of the guidance on how to develop an in-house Technology Architecture because they are heavy consumers of cloud services.

So, be prepared for questions on

Whether TOGAF® is to be adopted (Yes)

What is the adoption known as ? : (As Tailoring or as Customization)

What can be tailored ? (any relevant portion of TOGAF®, ADM or other Components which demand adaptation with other supplementing Frameworks (ITIL, PMP, COBIT or anything like these) or best practices; with other EA Frameworks (Zachman or other) and so on.

TOGAF® Standard can be used freely by any organization wishing to do so to develop an architecture for use within that organization. (Some licencing / membership terms with Open Group may apply)

---

77. https://pubs.opengroup.org/togaf-standard/architecture-content/chap06.html#tag_06_04_02

78. https://pubs.opengroup.org/togaf-standard/architecture-content/chap06.html#tag_06_06_01

79. https://pubs.opengroup.org/togaf-standard/architecture-content/chap06.html#tagfcjh_15

Is TOGAF® confined to IT centric Enterprises only ? (No. for any enterprise, including Government. For any section of any Enterprise)

The TOGAF® Standard is an open, industry consensus framework for Enterprise Architecture. It is a foundational framework, which means that it is applicable to the development of any kind of architecture in any context. This foundational framework is supplemented by The Open Group TOGAF® Library, an extensive and growing portfolio of guidance material, providing practical guidance in the application of the TOGAF® framework in specific contexts.

Note that apart from the TOGAF® Standard Fundamental Content, presented as six free-standing documents is in the Exam Syllabus for Level 1 and level 2, a few Series Guides also need to be studied. This Book Series reminds you about it at the appropriate places.

NON-CONVENTIONAL MULTIPLE choice questions start from here. Go through them with attention since such questions are hallmark of TOGAF® 10 Exam

Some questions here may involve other modules, especially those covered in this Book Series so far

Q 1350

Refer to the image below :

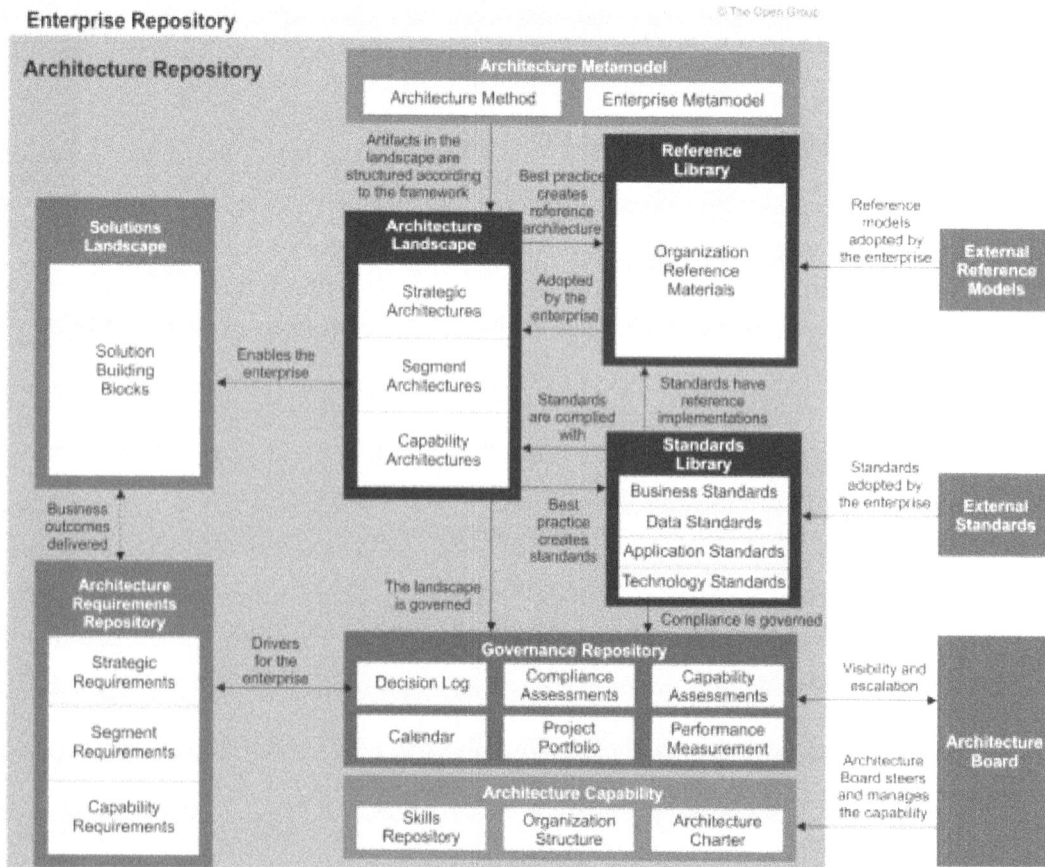

THE PORTIONS IN THIS repository store which are accessible in an indexed manner with the Enterprise Continuum and referred during Phases B to D are marked in

A. Green colour

B. Grey colour

C. Blue colour

D. None of the above

Explanation :

This is actually **Figure 6 : TOGAF® Architecture Repository**[80] **: Refer that for colours**

Read the details as given in **7.1 Overview**[81]

Look also into the structure of Enterprise Continuum[82]

Organization specific Architecture and Organization specific Solutions : these are stored in Architecture Landscape. Of these the three (blue coloured markings if you are seeing this in colour; in any case the ones named as : Architecture Landscape, Reference Library and Standards Library) are very often needed during Phases B to D, during which the ABB definition takes place.

Apart from the Architecture Landscape containing the Building Blocks produced and populated as and when the project progresses, other portions of the Enterprise Continuum needed in these phases are part of Reference Library or Standards Library. These are chosen by the Enterprise Architect and stored in the Repository in advance, as suitable.

These are what is shown as right hand side middle three boxes in the image of the question.

Answer : C

Q 1351

Pick the answer combination having right combination of True / False, on the following Statements on ADM and Iteration :

Statement

1 The ADM supports a number of concepts that are characterized as iteration.

2 Iteration describes the process of describing a comprehensive Architecture Landscape through multiple ADM cycles based upon individual initiatives bound to the scope of the Request for Architecture Work.

3 The idea of Iteration is used to describe the integrated process of developing an architecture where the activities described in different ADM phases counteract and contrast with each other to produce the architecture. In order to concisely describe the activity and outputs, this latter iteration is described in sequential terms.

4 TOGAF® reveals, in the context of partitions that : Iteration to develop a comprehensive Architecture Landscape : Projects will exercise through the entire ADM cycle, commencing with Phase A

A. 1 – True 2 – False 3 – True 4 – True

B. 1 – True 2 – True 3 – False 4 –True

80. https://pubs.opengroup.org/togaf-standard/adm-practitioners/adm-practitioners/adm-practitioners-7.png

81. https://pubs.opengroup.org/togaf-standard/architecture-content/chap07.html#tag_07_01

82. https://pubs.opengroup.org/togaf-standard/architecture-content/chap06.html#tagfcjh_15

C. 1 – False 2 – True 3 – True 4 – False

D. 1 – True 2 – True 3 – True 4 – False

Explanation :

See : **2.1 Overview**[83] : Applying the ADM part of TOGAF® Standard Fundamental Content Version 10

Row 3) should have been :

The idea of ... of developing ... where the .. **interact to produce** ....

In order to ..., this latter iteration is ....

Note that as long as integrated architecture is kept as the focus, interaction needs between Phases give scope for the iterative flow.

Answer : B

Q 1352 : HINT

Be prepared for questions on multiple ADM cycles. While it is mandatory to go through each Phase at least once, there are no rigid stipulations about the iterative flow between Phases. Same Phase may be visited multiple times. Preliminary Phase is only one that is visited rarely, if at all needed, that too only from Phase A

Q 1353 : Hint

Be prepared for questions on the integration need and the possibilities of flow paths.

Main point to note is that iteration describes the process of managing change to the organization's Architecture Capability. That is why Strategic Partition leads to segmental approach and finally into Incremental Capability partition.

Q 1354 : Hint

Be prepared for questions which anchor upon on ADM cycle that starts in Phase A. Note that Preliminary Phase is not part of the cycle, but a once in a while activity.

Q 1355

Pick the answer combination having right combination of True / False, on the following Statements on ADM and Iteration :

Statement

1 Each cycle of the ADM will be bound by a Request for Architecture Work. The architecture output will populate the Architecture Landscape, either extending the landscape described, or changing the landscape where required.

2 Separate projects may operate their own ADM cycles, but not concurrently, with relationships between the different projects.

One project may trigger the initiation of another project.

3 Typically, this is used when higher-level architecture initiatives identify opportunities or solutions that require more detailed architecture, or when a project identifies landscape impacts outside the scope of its Request for Architecture Work.

4 TOGAF® reveals, in the context of partitions that : Iteration to develop a comprehensive Architecture Landscape : Projects will exercise through the entire ADM cycle, commencing with Phase A.

A. 1 – True 2 – False 3 – True 4 – True

B. 1 – True 2 – True 3 – False 4 –True

C. 1 – False 2 – True 3 – True 4 – False

D. 1 – True 2 – True 3 – True 4 – False

Explanation :

See : **2.1 Overview**[84] : Applying the ADM part of TOGAF® Standard Fundamental Content Version 10

Statement 2) should have been :

Separate projects may ... cycles, **but concurrently**, with ... projects.

One project may trigger the ...

Answer : A

―――――――――

Q 1356 : HINT

Be prepared for questions which relate Request for Architecture Work (Preliminary Phase) to work in subsequent Phases

Same way, be prepared for relate Statement of Architecture Work (Phase A) to work in subsequent Phases

Note from above how a project may have own ADM cycle and many concurrent ADM cycles are possible.

This implies that many concurrent projects may find common services, as discovered in Phase E

---

84. https://pubs.opengroup.org/togaf-standard/applying-the-adm/chap02.html#tag_02_01

Q 1357

Pick the answer combination having right combination of True / False, on the following Statements on ADM and Iteration :

Statement

TOGAF® emphasizes in this connection that : Iteration within an ADM cycle (Architecture Development iteration) :

1 Projects may operate multiple ADM phases concurrently

Typically, this is used to manage the inter-relationship between Business Architecture, Information Systems Architecture, and Technology Architecture

Projects cannot return to previous phases to update work products with new information

2 Typically, this is used to converge on an executable Architecture Roadmap or Implementation and Migration Plan, when the implementation details and scope of change trigger a change or re-prioritization of stakeholder requirements.

Projects may cycle between ADM phases, in planned cycles covering multiple phases.

3 Typically, this is used to converge on a detailed Target Architecture when higher-level architecture does not exist to provide context and constraint.

4 TOGAF® reveals, in the context of partitions that : Iteration to develop a comprehensive Architecture Landscape : Projects will exercise through the entire ADM cycle, commencing with Phase A

A. 1 – True 2 – False 3 – True 4 – True

B. 1 – True 2 – True 3 – False 4 –True

C. 1 – False 2 – True 3 – True 4 – False

D. 1 – True 2 – True 3 – True 4 – False

Explanation :

See : **2.1 Overview**[85] : Applying the ADM part of TOGAF® Standard Fundamental Content Version 10

Statement 2) should have been :

... may **return to previous phases** to ... with new ..

Typically, this is used to .. Roadmap .. Plan, when the ... and scope of .. a ... of ....

Answer : A

Q 1358 : HINT

Be prepared for questions on aspects such as :

Iteration to manage the Architecture Capability (Architecture Capability iteration) :

---

85. https://pubs.opengroup.org/togaf-standard/applying-the-adm/chap02.html#tag_02_01

Projects may require a new iteration of the Preliminary Phase to (re-)establish aspects of the Architecture Capability identified in Phase A to address a Request for Architecture Work. Projects may require a new iteration of the Preliminary Phase to adjust the organization's Architecture Capability as a result of identifying new or changed requirements for Architecture Capability or as a result of a Change Request in Phase H. This is mentioned above as occasional revisit to Preliminary Phase

Q 1359 : Hint

Be prepared for questions on aspects such as : Refer to : **Figure 2-1 Iteration Cycles**[86] : 2.2 : Iteration Cycles[87] : 2. Applying Iteration to the ADM under Applying the ADM part of TOGAF® Standard Fundamental Content Version 10

While studying the figure above, (known as crop-circle diagram) also note from : **5.2 How is ADM Iteration Realized in Practice**[88] in TOGAF® Series Guide : A Practitioners' Approach to Developing Enterprise Architecture Following the TOGAF® ADM :

The TOGAF® ADM graphic provides a ... that is often misinterpreted as a ....

The TOGAF® ADM is a logical method that places ... information flow.

The classic TOGAF® crop-circle diagram is a .... essential information flow.

The TOGAF® ADM should not be understood as a .... T

he ADM graphic is ... useful outputs.

Depending on what a Practitioner is requested to develop, an ... will vary.

Q 1360 : Hint

Be prepared for questions on aspects from yet another Series Guide on **digital Transformation**[89] :

The TOGAF® Standard supports ... to become a digital enterprise.

It is important to consider that ... is also a plus.

The TOGAF® Standard can be used to .. products, and to ... excellence.

The TOGAF® ADM provides ... be described as solution architectures

Using guidance available in the TOGAF® Standard, the ... and "right-sized" for smaller or less complex environments.

---

86. https://pubs.opengroup.org/togaf-standard/applying-the-adm/chap02.html#tagfcjh_1

87. https://pubs.opengroup.org/togaf-standard/applying-the-adm/chap02.html#tag_02_02

88. https://pubs.opengroup.org/togaf-standard/adm-practitioners/adm-practitioners_5.html#_Toc95288832

89. https://pubs.opengroup.org/togaf-standard/guides/using-the-togaf-standard-in-the-digital-enterprise/index.html

Q 1361

Refer to the table below :

Phase	Output & Outcome	Essential Knowledge
?	A set of domain architectures approved by the stakeholders for the problem being addressed, with a set of gaps, and work to clear the gaps understood by the stakeholders.	How does the current Enterprise fail to meet the preferences of the stakeholders ? What must change to enable the Enterprise to meet the preferences of the stakeholders ? (Gaps) What work is necessary to realize the changes, that is consistent with the additional value being created ? (Work Package) How stakeholder priority and preference adjust in response to value, effort, and risk of change. (Stakeholder Requirements)

Which ADM phase(s) does this describe?

A. Preliminary Phase and Phase A

B. Phases B, C and D

C. Phase E

D. Phase F

Explanation :

Go through : **5.2.2 Essential ADM Output and Knowledge**[90] along with **Table 4 : Essential ADM Outputs, Outcomes, and Knowledge**[91] from TOGAF® Series Guide : A Practitioners' Approach to Developing Enterprise Architecture

Do note that Work Packages in the form of ABB centric grouping my start evolving in Phases C and D. However Work Packages based on delivery vehicle is firmed up only in Phase E. Do see the next row on Phase E in the same table.

Answer : B

---

90. https://pubs.opengroup.org/togaf-standard/adm-practitioners/adm-practitioners_5.html#_Toc95288834

91. https://pubs.opengroup.org/togaf-standard/adm-practitioners/adm-practitioners_5.html#_Ref490978563

Q 1362

Refer to the table below :

Essential Knowledge Column 1	Essential Knowledge Column 2
	How does the current Enterprise fail to meet the preferences of the stakeholders ?
The scope of the problem being addressed.	
Those who have interests that are fundamental to the problem being addressed. (Stakeholders & Concerns)	What must change to enable the Enterprise to meet the preferences of the stakeholders ? (Gaps)
What summary answer to the problem is acceptable to the stakeholders?	What work is necessary to realize the changes, that is consistent with the additional value being created ? (Work Package)
Stakeholder priority and preference.	
What value does the summary answer provide?	How stakeholder priority and preference adjust in response to value, effort, and risk of change. (Stakeholder Requirements)

   A. Column 1 is about Phase A; Column 2 is about Phases B to D
   B. Column 1 is about Phase B; Column 2 is about Phase A
   C. Column 1 is about Preliminary Phase; Column 2 is about Phases B to D
   D. Column 1 is about Phase C; Column 2 is about Phases B to D

Explanation :

Go through : **5.2.2 Essential ADM Output and Knowledge**[92] along with **Table 4 : Essential ADM Outputs, Outcomes, and Knowledge**[93] from TOGAF® Series Guide : A Practitioners' Approach to Developing Enterprise Architecture

Answer : A

---

92. https://pubs.opengroup.org/togaf-standard/adm-practitioners/adm-practitioners_5.html#_Toc95288834

93. https://pubs.opengroup.org/togaf-standard/adm-practitioners/adm-practitioners_5.html#_Ref490978563

Q 1363

Refer to the image below, which is adapted from one of Open Group :

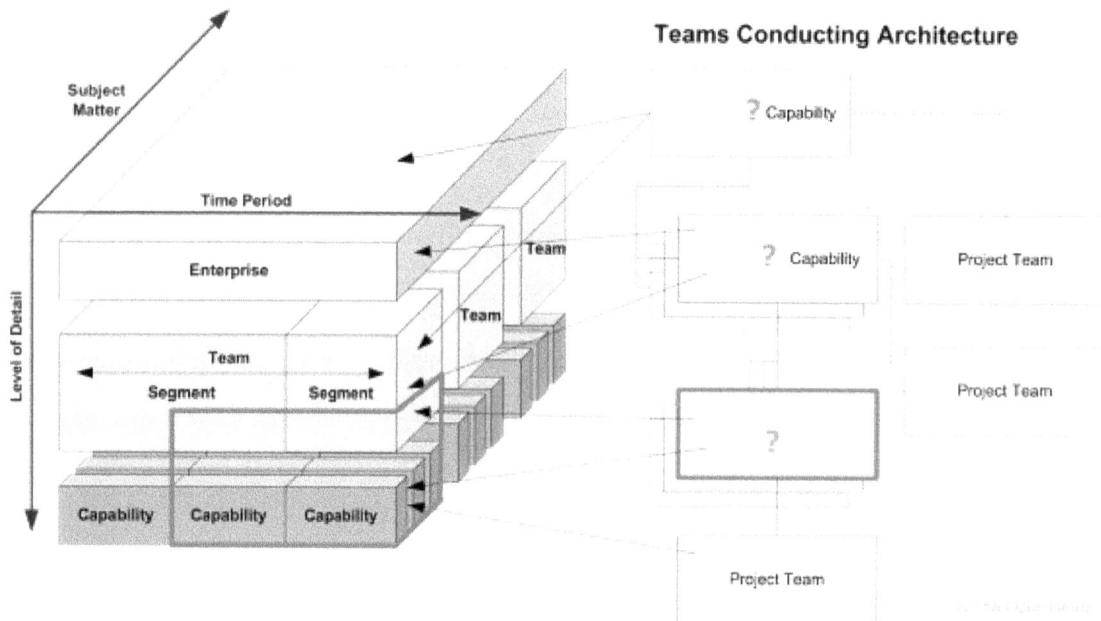

PICK THE RIGHT ANSWER for the three Team details shown as **? , ? and ? one below the other vertically**

- A. **?** = Architecture **?** = Design **?** = Implementation
- B. **?** = Enterprise **?** = Vision **?** = Execution
- C. **?** = Corporate EA **?** = Segment EA **?** = Portfolio Team
- D. **?** = Enterprise EA **?** = Transition EA **?** = Operations Team

Explanation :

See : **4.2.1 Activities within the Preliminary Phase**[94] : **Figure 4-1 : Allocation of Teams to Architecture Scope**[95] : Applying the ADM part of TOGAF® Standard Fundamental Content Version 10

Go through the entire section for additional knowledge.

Answer : C

94. https://pubs.opengroup.org/togaf-standard/applying-the-adm/chap04.html#tag_04_02_01

95. https://pubs.opengroup.org/togaf-standard/applying-the-adm/chap04.html#tagfcjh_8

Looking at Official Level 1 Syllabus of Unit 7 – Architecture Content

Remembering Level Expected, through definitions, list of things involved or basic description of

TOGAF® Standard deliverables created and consumed in different TOGAF® ADM phases (covered under respective phases to some extent and is consolidated here as :

Architecture Contract

Architecture Definition Document

Architecture Principles

Architecture Requirements Specification

Architecture Roadmap

Architecture Vision

Business Principles, Business Goals, and Business Drivers

Capability Assessment

Change Request

Communications Plan

Compliance Assessment

Implementation and Migration Plan

Implementation Governance Model

Request for Architecture Work

Requirements Impact Assessment

Statement of Architecture Work

Understanding Level of due explanation and summarization is expected in the following :

Key concepts: stakeholders, concerns, architecture views, architecture viewpoints, and their relationships; what Building Blocks are and their use in the ADM. (Seen in Module 6)

You may like to know the Exam syllabus relating to **Unit 5 – Introduction to Applying the ADM** :

Remembering Level Expected, through definitions, list of things involved or basic description of :

Guidance on how to apply the TOGAF® Standard

Understanding Level is Expected in the following :

How iteration within the ADM enables concurrent operation of multiple ADM phases.

Three levels of the Architecture Landscape

How partitioning helps simplify the development of an Enterprise Architecture

Four purposes that help to frame the planning horizon and breadth and depth of the Architecture Project

How the TOGAF® Standard can be applied to support the Digital enterprise

About the various Book Series available from the same Author :

The 9.2 Certification is kept open even as TOGAF 10 Certification has started. Might remain so for quite a few months ahead

———

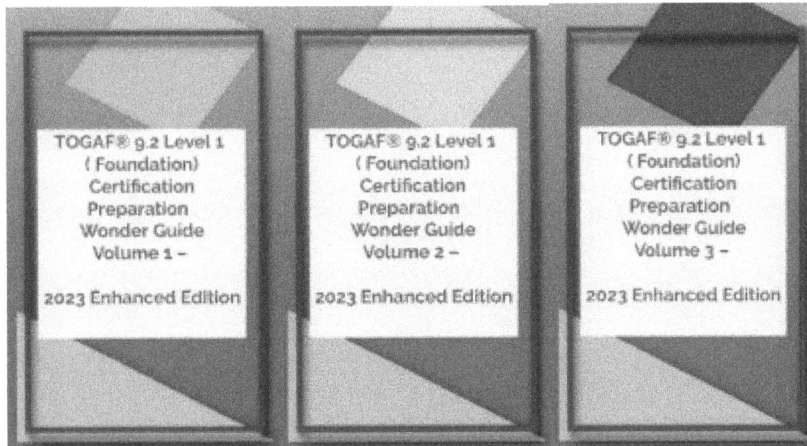

The three volumes together make up for your preparation for Level 1 Exam –

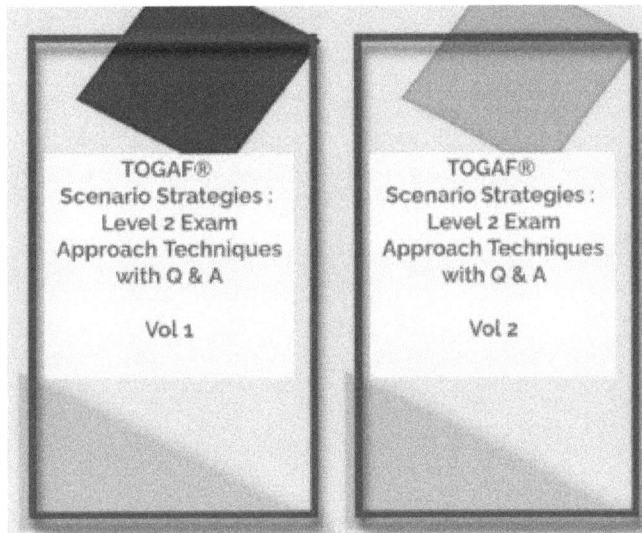

The two volumes together makes up for your preparation for Level 2 Exam

Ideally TOGAF® 10 can be approached with a One hour exam, if you possess TOGAF® 9.2 or TOGAF® 9.1 Certification

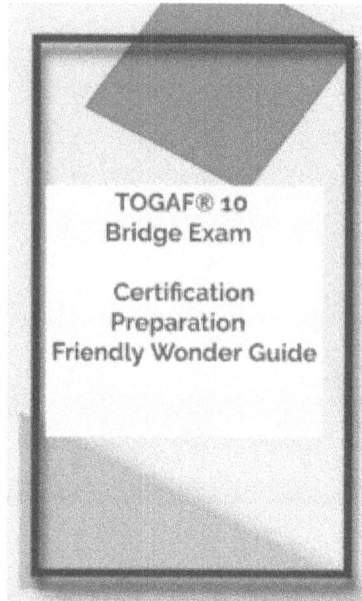

AND FOR THOSE WHO WANT to take TOGAF® 10 fresh, :

AS ALSO VOLUMES ON Level 2 tilted as Scenario Strategies for TOGAF® 10 Exam

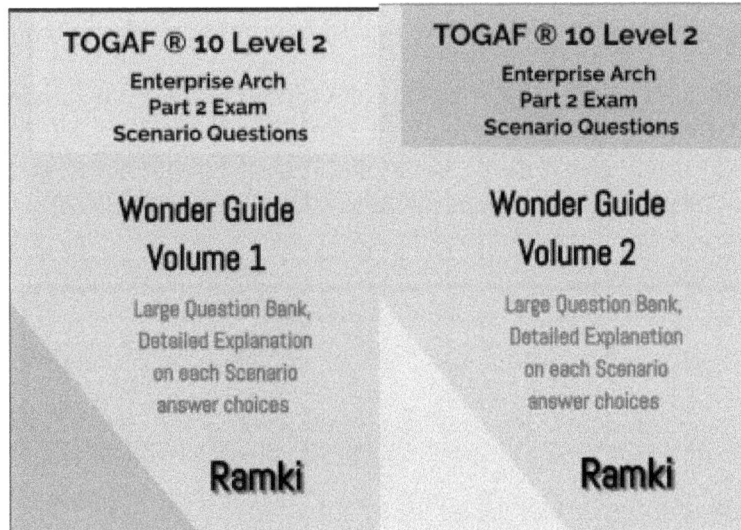

Author & Expert Faculty : Ramakrishnan N (Ramki)

———

Ramki is the pen name of Ramakrishnan N. This author has nearly 50 years of experience and exposure in the field of IT, and most of it is attributed to Software Architecture. He has seen the advent of this specialist field of Software Architecture over the years and is still in good touch with all modern evolution of the same.

TOGAF® 10 places more focussed approach of Enterprise Architecture getting into areas such as :

- Microservice Architecture
- Digital Enterprise and Digital Technology Adoption : Digital Business Reference Model (DBRM)
- Information Mapping and Organization Mapping
- Customer Master Data Management (C-MDM)
- TOGAF® ADM using Agile Sprints

These happen to be the precise areas where the author has equipped himself with practical and conceptual knowledge.

Books of same author, Ramki, as TOGAF® Certification Wonder Books (three volumes for Level 1 and one for Level 2 – Scenario Strategies) have been admired and being purchased by hundreds on a day to day basis.

Books on Design Patterns and other Architectural topics are also to the credit of this author.

He has also provided training to participants from a large number of Enterprises spanning all over the globe. The number of participants to his TOGAF® courses alone is close to 2000 as of the year 2022.

Reachable through: mramkiz@gmail.com

9 798223 721499